JESUS
(God, Man, Myth)

JESUS
(God, Man, Myth)

J. Harvey Hames

ReadersMagnet, LLC

Jesus: (God, Man, Myth)
Copyright © 2021 by J. Harvey Hames

Published in the United States of America
ISBN Paperback: 978-1-954371-23-1
ISBN eBook: 978-1-954371-24-8

All rights reserved. No part of this publication may be reproduced, stored in a retrieval system or transmitted in any way by any means, electronic, mechanical, photocopy, recording or otherwise without the prior permission of the author except as provided by USA copyright law.

ReadersMagnet, LLC
10620 Treena Street, Suite 230 | San Diego, California, 92131 USA
1.619.354.2643 | www.readersmagnet.com

Book design copyright © 2021 by ReadersMagnet, LLC. All rights reserved.
Cover design by Ericka Obando
Interior design by Renalie Malinao

In this book you will read things you have NEVER thought or heard before. That does NOT mean they are NOT TRUE. OPEN YOU MIND!

(This book is my opinion. YOU CREATE YOUR OWN OPINION). Many things will be of a Spiritual world. JUST OPEN YOUR MIND TO NEW THINKING.

"This might be the most important book I have ever written."

One time while praying, I asked Jesus; who are You? I deeply wanted to know who Jesus really was.

This book is not being written to praise Harvey.
It is being written to glorify the
Lord Jesus Christ,
the Son of God.

If you want to know Jesus, maybe before you finish reading this book, you will know Him the way I know Him NOW. The most momentous reason is Jesus was and is God's Son. The Man above all others, wonderful, kind, powerful and He is EVERYTHING. No other Man like Him has ever lived on earth.

Just to let you know this is my opinion. (YOU MUST CREATE YOUR OWN). There will be many things I write in this book that will make you say, "what"? They might seem like they are from another world. They will be--a Spiritual world. PLEASE JUST TRY AND KEEP YOUR MIND OPEN TO NEW THINGS.

In all my books there will be things you have NEVER been taught or thought of before. Trust me, that does NOT mean they are NOT TRUE. THAT MEANS YOU WILL HAVE TO STUDY YOUR BIBLE TO PROVE THEY ARE TRUE OR NOT TRUE.

You see, there are thousands and millions of books written about Jesus. There is just ONE Jesus. The bookstores, libraries and internet are filled with books about just ONE Jesus. Thank about that.

Paul said in I Timothy 2:5:

"FOR THERE IS ONE GOD, and ONE MEDIATOR BETWEEN GOD and MAN, the MAN CHRIST JESUS".

I CANNOT TEACH anybody anything I CAN ONLY MAKE them THINK (Socrates).

So many different thoughts about the same Jesus. Many men and women have spent countless hours studying the Bible. If I wanted to tell you EVERYTHING about Jesus or the Bible, I would have to write hundreds and thousands of pages. Even then I could not tell you EVERYTHING about Jesus. This is not that type of book. In this book I want to tell you details you would NOT see in the other books. My goal is to get you to think about the Bible in a way that you would WANT to study the Bible MORE and MORE every day. The main theme in all the Bible spoken of from Genesis to Revelation is "JESUS".

When I read about John Milton, the poet, that wrote: Pilgrim's Progress; "When I think of how my life is spent air half my days in this dark world and wide. And that ONE talent which is death to hide lodged with me useless thou my soul more bent to serve there with my Maker and present my true account, less He, returning chide. Does God exact day labor light denied I fondly ask, but patience to prevent that mummer soon replied. God does not exact day labor light denied. They serve Him best who bare His mild yolk. Thousands at His bidding speed post over land and ocean without rest. They also serve Him who only stand and wait".

You see, John Milton was blind, and he did not use his talent, writing poetry, until he was halfway through his life. He must have thought it was death to not use your talent.

God please help me to use ANY talent I might have.

James 1:5, "If any of you lack wisdom, let him ask of God, that giveth to all men liberally, and upbraid not; and it shall be given him".

God please give me your WISDOM to write this book that is titled "Jesus".

Have you ever gone to a circus only to see a giant elephant with a small rope around one of its back leg? The elephant could break the rope at any time. However, the elephant has been conditioned. When it was very, young they had a large chain around the same leg. The elephant tried but could not break it. He became conditioned. He does not even try to break it now because he is conditioned. Many of us are like that. We have thought a certain way and refuse to think any different. I hope and pray we are not CONDITIONED.

I am trying to free your mind, but I can only show you the door. You are the one that must walk through it.

Education is not the learning of facts, but the training of the mind to think (Einstein).

Why do we close our eyes when we pray, cry, kiss or dream? Because all the "spiritual" things in life are NOT seen but felt only with our heart.

As I mentioned earlier, while praying, I ask Jesus "Who are You?", and He answered me as to who He was. Now I know Him better and closer than I hav.e EVER known Him in my life. Before you come to the end of this book, I also hope you can get closer to Jesus and see Him in a brighter light.

"All quotations from King James Translation"

Is Jesus a Myth?

In the title of this book, I posted three questions. Was Jesus, GOD? Was Jesus JUST a MAN? Is Jesus a MYTH?

OK, I see why a few of you feel Jesus is a myth. Jesus NEVER wrote a book, (yet all the libraries of this country could be filled with books written about Him). He NEVER marshalled an army, fired a gun, (yet He made more men lay down their arms without a shot being fired). He NEVER practiced medicine, (yet He healed the multitudes and did not charged for His services).

We do NOT even have a real picture or painting of Jesus. We know the year but NOT the exact day or time He was born. Yet millions of people believe in Jesus. Why do you think that is? I feel Jesus wants us to accept Him by faith. Even now how many people do you see wearing a necklace, that is a cross? Jesus does not want us to have any idols before us.

If you believe Jesus is a myth, why do you believe it? I see. You need more proof. It has been about two thousand years since Jesus lived on earth. At this point, I am not sure I can show you more proof than you already have.

Is Jesus just a myth? 99% of our history books say Jesus was a real Man that lived here on earth for approximately 33 years. We also have other writers, not in the Bible, that wrote about Jesus during the time of Jesus. One was Josephus. Read his writings. He says Jesus was NOT a myth.

Think of all the men that wrote books in the New Testament. All of them saw and heard Jesus. Even the Apostle Paul had an experience with Jesus. The twelve Apostles ate, sleep and traveled with Jesus. They touched and spoke to Jesus. Jesus was NOT a myth. Jesus was a real man that lived here on earth for 33 years. Thousands of people saw and talked to Jesus. Thousands of people were healed by Jesus. Try and tell all those people that Jesus is a myth.

Maybe we should talk about Jesus, just being a man, and not able to do all the things written about Him in the Bible? If you do not believe in Jesus, do you believe He lived here on earth for 33 years? Can you admit that

Jesus was a real man that lived here on earth for 33 years? Okay, now let us build on that.

If only I could be with you, to find out what you do believe about Jesus.

Yes, there are a lot of things we do not know exactly about Jesus. However, is that a reason to say He is a Myth? Sorry, but I am just trying to get in your head and see what you really believe.

Maybe one of the reasons you keep telling yourself He is a Myth, because you do not want to accept Jesus as your personal Savior. That I could understand. Maybe you feel you will have to stop doing the things you are doing now. Yes, the things you feel are bring pleasure and enjoyment to your life.

I feel you have not had an experience with Jesus so you might feel He is a myth.

I do not want to tell you how to live. How to eat. How to take care of your body. How not to lust after a woman, man or riches. How you should not destroy your own body. I want you to know, that I am not trying to tell you, that you cannot think like this or that or any other way.

If you want to say Jesus is a Myth, go ahead. However, you will KNOW deep down in your heart that He is NOT a myth.

You might say, if Jesus is so important, why do we NOT even have a picture or painting of Him? Jesus wants you to except Him by faith. The Bible tells us that BLESSED is the person that believes in Jesus that has never seen, heard or talked with Him.

After you read this book, then please answer the question; "Do you feel that Jesus is a Myth?"

There are a lot of things we do NOT know about Jesus, but there are a lot of things we do know about Jesus. If you truly, think Jesus is a MYTH, I hope by the time you finish reading this book that you will KNOW JESUS IS REAL.

I know nothing with certainty, but the sight of the stars, make me dream. (Vincent van Gogh)

Meditation is Medication…

A single word spoken at the right time could change someone's life forever.

Was Jesus JUST a Man?

Now to the second question. Was Jesus JUST a Man that lived on earth approximately 2,000 years ago? Yes, Jesus was a man that lived here on earth about 2,000 years ago. However, he was not just a man like you and me.

Jesus was born in Bethlehem during the last years of Herod the Great (St Matthew 1:18 to 25 and St Luke 2:1 to 7). Jesus, at His birth, was acclaimed God's Chosen One (St Luke 2:8 to 21). As an infant, Jesus was circumcised. Then later at the days of purification at the temple in Jerusalem, in keeping with Jewish custom (St Luke 2:22 to 39). Wise men from the East presented Him with gifts of gold, frankincense and myrrh (St Matthew 2:11-12).

Warned by an angel that King Herod was jealous of His rival and had ordered the massacre of all male infants. Joseph and Mary rushed Jesus to safety in Egypt (St Matthew 2:13 to 23). Jesus and His family remained in Egypt until Herod's death. Then they moved to Nazareth in Galilee.

The Bible does not give us another record of Jesus until He was twelve years old (St Luke 2:41 to 52). We do not know anything of His young Boyhood. However, at twelve Joseph and Mary took Jesus and a lot of relatives to Jerusalem for the feast of the Passover which was their custom. When they had fulfilled the days of the Passover, they were on their way home for about a day's journey. Then they realized that Jesus was not with their company of people. Jesus tarried behind in Jerusalem. When they noticed Jesus was not amount their company of people, Mary and Joseph returned to Jerusalem.

Three days had passed before they found Him in the Temple sitting in the middle of doctors and priests. Jesus was both hearing them and asking them questions.

St Luke 2:47 "And all that heard Him were astonished at His understanding and answers."

When Joseph and Mary saw Him, they were amazed. Mary said, Son, we have been looking for you everywhere.

(48) "And when they saw Him, they were amazed: and His mother said unto Him, Son, why hast thou dealt with us? Behold thy father and I have sought thee

sorrowing. (49) And He said unto them, 'how is it that ye sought me? Know ye not that I must be about My Father's business'?"

They did not understand what Jesus was saying to them. Then Jesus returned with them to Nazareth, but Mary kept these sayings in her heart.

St Luke 2:52 "And Jesus increased in wisdom and stature, and favor with God and man".

Jesus was in Nazareth where He was mainly brought up. It was early in His ministry and all the people around Him knew He was the Son of Mary, and THEY THOUGHT JOSEPH. JESUS WAS NOT THE SON OF JOSEPH. Yes, Joseph raised Him. JESUS WAS NOT THE SON OF JOSEPH, BUT <u>HE WAS AND IS THE SON OF GOD</u>.

John the Baptist had started his ministry. As a young man Jesus went to John to be baptized, and John said I am unworthy to Baptist You. Jesus insisted on John baptizing Him and he did (St Matthew 3:13 to 17; St Luke 3:21 to 23). Please read these verses.

St Mark 1:9-10-11 "It came to pass in those days, that Jesus came from Nazareth of Galilee, and was baptized of John the Baptist in Jordan. (10) And straightway coming up out of the water, He saw the Heavens opened, and the Spirit like a dove descending upon Him. (11)

And there came a voice from Heaven, saying; 'Thou art My believed Son, in whom I am well pleased'."

Then Jesus withdrew into the wilderness to pray and think about His mission as the Son of God.

When He did, the devil temped Jesus three times, but Jesus overcame all the temptations. Yes, Jesus was temped in all ways just as we are, yet without sin. It is spelled out in (St Matthew 4:1 to 11; St Luke 4:1 to 13). St Mark 1:12-13:

(12) "And immediately the Spirit drives Him (Jesus) into the wilderness. (13) And He was there in the wilderness forty days, tempted of Satan; and was with the wild beasts; and the angels ministered unto Him."

People asked Jesus for help in His village.

St Mark 6:4-5-6 "Jesus said unto them, a prophet is not without honor, but in His own country, and amount His own kin, and in His own house. (5) And He could there do no mighty work, save that He laid His hands upon a few sick people, and healed them. (6) And He marveled because of their unbelief. And He went round about the villages, teaching."

Yes, Jesus was a man, but NOT just a Man. The people there had known Jesus from boyhood and DID NOT believe He could work miracles. People MUST believe.

Remember the time Jesus and His 12 disciples came to a lady's house and her daughter was sick unto death? Jesus took only a few with Him inside to pray, because of their un-belief.

LUKE 8:51 to 56 "When He came into the house, He suffered NO man to go in, save Peter, and James, and John, and the father and the mother of the maiden. (52) And all wept, and bewailed her; but He said, 'weep not', she is not dead, but is sleeping. (53) And they laughed Him to scorn, knowing that she was dead. (54) And He PUT THEM ALL OUT, and took her by the hand and called, saying, 'maid arise'. (55) And her spirit came again, and she arose straightway; and He commanded to give her meat. (56) And her parents were astonished; but He charged them that they should tell no man what was done."

You see the people in Nazareth thought they knew Jesus, so they DID NOT believe. If they had only KNOWN who Jesus really was?

We are still like that today. You do not believe, because you do not KNOW who Jesus really is. Think positive. If your negative channel is on—change it. Do NOT believe things that are not true.

Remember St John 2:1-5 "And the third day there was a marriage in Cana of Galilee, and the mother of Jesus was there; (2) and, both Jesus was called, and His disciples, to the marriage. (3) And when they wanted wine, the mother of Jesus saith unto Him. They have no wine. (4) Jesus saith unto her (His mother), 'woman what have I to do with thee? Mine hour is not yet come'. (5) His mother saith unto the servants, 'whatsoever He saith unto you, do it'."

Please let me point out several things. This was the first miracle we know that Jesus performed. Jesus said His hour had not yet come to start His ministry. Jesus had already chosen some of His disciples because they were with Him. Jesus knew there were unbelievers there. And last, Jesus said to His mother, "woman what have I to do with you?" I do not know about you, but if I said to my mother, "woman what have I to do with you?" Whooooo… Jesus must have been uncomfortable with Mary asking Him to perform a miracle at that time.

You MUST read St John 2:6 to 11. Jesus gave them plenty of wine. A FIEKIN is about nine gallons. There were six pots, and they could hold two to three FIEKINS each. That is 18 to 27 gallons times SIX equals 108 to 162 gallons of new wine. Do you think you could complete a wedding party with that much wine? I believe Jesus made that much wine at this party because His mother ASKED Him to work a miracle. However, Jesus always gives with abundance.

I do not know of anyone in my lifetime that was able to change water into wine, and especially that much wine. Do you know of anyone?

This is just one thing that Jesus did. There are hundreds of things in the Bible. There are thousands of things that were not written in the Bible that Jesus did.

For one minute, walk outside, stand there, in silence, look up at the sky, and contemplate how amazing life is.

After the temptation of the devil in the wilderness, Jesus returned to Nazareth.

St Luke 4:16 to 21 "He came to Nazareth where He had been brought up. And as His custom was, He went into the synagogue on the sabbath day, and stood up for to read. (17) And there was delivered unto Him the book of the prophet Esaias. And when He had opened the book, He found the place where it was written. (18) The Spirit of the Lord is upon me, because He hath anointed me to preach the gospel to the poor; He hath sent Me to heal the brokenhearted, to preach deliverance to the captives, and recovering of sight to the blind, to set at liberty them that are bruised. (19) To preach the acceptable year of the Lord. (20) And He closed the book, and He gave it again to the minister, and sat down. And the eyes of ALL them that were in the synagogue were fastened on Him. (21) And He began to say unto them, this day is this scripture fulfilled in your ears."

Can you imagine what was going through their minds at that time? What do you think they were saying among themselves? One of the things they, said; is not this Joseph's Son? If they only knew He was NOT Joseph's son, but Jesus the <u>SON of GOD</u>. He was NOT the Son of Joseph, but the SON OF GOD.

Verse (24) says; "And Jesus said, verily I say unto you, 'no prophet is accepted in his own country'."

Jesus said God sent Elias to Sidon to help Sarepts, a widow, after a great famine for three years and six months. Even thou there were many people that needed healing, God sent Elias just to help her.

St Luke 4:28-29-30 "And all they in the synagogue, when they hear these things, were filled with wrath. (29) And rose up, and thrust Him out of the city, and led Him unto the brow of the hill whereon their city was built, that they might cast Him down headlong. (30) But He, passing through the midst of them, went His way."

Then we find Jesus calling some of His first disciples from His audiences of fishermen near Capernaum by the sea of Galilee (St Matthew 4:18 to 22). All that He chose immediately followed Him.

Jesus was very well known among the common people. However, He begin to encounter hostility among the religious leaders. Especially when He and His disciples plucked corn and healed the sick on the

Sabbath. Jesus said, if you had a lamb in a ditch on the Sabbath, would you not help it out? At this point, they were trying to catch Jesus doing ANYTHING so they could accuse Him. Knowing their hostility, I believe Jesus tried to teach His followers the responsibilities of the kingdom of God (St Matthew 5, 6 and 7).

Jesus also taught them by parables. When Jesus would set on the seaside, great multitudes would gather. So many until He had to go on a boat and let them stand on the shore. He would teach them with simple parables that they could understand.

Jesus' disciples came to Jesus and asked, why do you teach the multitudes with parables?

St Matthew 13:11 to 15; "He answered and said unto them, because it is given unto you to know the MYSTERIES of the kingdom of Heaven, but to them it is not given. (12) For whosoever hath, to him shall be given, and he shall have more abundance; but whosoever hath not, from him shall be taken away even that he hath. (13) Therefore, speak I to them in parables: because they, seeing, see not; and hearing they hear not, neither do they understand. (15) For this people's heart is waxed gross, and their ears are dull of hearing, and their eyes they have closed; lest at any time they should see with their eyes and hear with their ears, and should understand with their heart, and should be converted, and I SHOULD HEAL THEM."

In St Matthew 13:11 Jesus said that His disciples would "know the MYSTERIES OF THE KINGDOM OF HEAVEN", but the multitudes would not understand. That is the reason He also spoke to His disciples in parables.

I knew you would be curious about the meaning of this. This is something you need to help me with. I have looked up all the verses about the MYSTERIES. Now open your Bible and read what it says.

1. The MYSTERIES of the kingdom of Heaven (Mark 13:3 to 27).

2. The MYSTERY of Israel's blindness during this age (Romans 11:25).

3. The MYSTERY of the translation of living saints at the end of this age (I Thessalonians 4:13-17 must read).

4. The MYSTERY of the New Testament church as one body composed of Jew and Gentile (Ephesians 3:1 to 11).

5. The MYSTERY of the church as the bride of Christ (Ephesians 5:27 to 32).

6. The MYSTERY of the in-living Christ (Galatians 2:20).

7. The MYSTERY of Christ as the incarnate fullness of the Godhead embodied, in all the

divine wisdom for man subsists (Colossians 2:2 to 10). (Verses 9 & 10 MUST READ).

8. The MYSTERY of the processes by which Godlikeness is restored in man (I Timothy 3:16).
9. The MYSTERY of iniquity (Mark 13:32-33).
10. The MYSTERY of the seven stars (Revelation 1:20).
11. The MYSTERY of Babylon (Revelation 17:5 & 9).

Number 7 above says in Colossians 2:9:

"For in Jesus dwelleth all the fulness of the Godhead Bodily."

How could the apostle Paul have made these MYSTERIES more, clear?

In studying for this book, I found things in the Bible I did not remember reading before.

Dear PAST, thank you for all the lessons. Dear FUTURE, I am ready for anything.

It does not matter if the glass is half empty or half full. Be grateful that you have a glass with something in it.

We are still on the chapter; WAS JESUS JUST A MAN?

As I asked before, "Was Jesus Just a Man," here on earth for 33 years? Was Jesus only like a Man? Jesus was MUCH MORE than any other man that HAS EVER LIVED ON THIS EARTH.

You CAN BELIEVE whatever you want, but you really NEED TO BELIEVE IN JESUS.

Jesus had gone to Bethsaida and healed many of the people. He also was teaching them. Then the day was coming to an end, and the twelve disciples came to Jesus and said send the people home so they could get something to eat. Also find a place to sleep. Jesus said to the twelve, "feed them". They said all we have are five loaves of bread and two fishes. There are about five thousand men plus women and children here. Jesus said have them set down in groups of fifty. The disciples sat them in groups of fifty. Then they gave the five loaves and two fishes to Jesus to pray over. Jesus gave the food to His twelve disciples in baskets. Then Jesus said feed them. The disciples feed ALL the multitude, and they were ALL filled. Then Jesus said pick up the fragments that are left. "Remember, they were ALL filled".

Jesus asked them to pick up the leftovers. They filled twelve baskets with what was left over. Jesus always gives more than is needed with His abundance.

Mark 5:25 to 34 another miracle of Jesus: (25) "And a certain woman, which had an issue of blood twelve years, (26) And had suffered many things of many physicians, and had spent ALL that she had, and was nothing bettered, but rather grew worse. (28) For she said, if I may touch but His clothes, I shall be whole. (29) And straightway the fountain of her blood was dried up; and she felt in her body that she was healed of that plague. (30) And Jesus immediately knowing in Himself that virtue had gone out of Him."

Jesus turns and said, "who touched Me?" His disciples said the multitude surrounds You, and You say, who touched Me? But the woman fearing and trembling and knowing what she had done, came and fell-down before Him, and told what she had done. (34) "And He said unto her, daughter, <u>YOUR FAITH HATH MADE YOU WHOLE</u>; go in peace and be whole of thy plague."

St Matthew 9:18 another miracle:

(18) "While He yet spoke these things to them, behold, there came a certain RULER, and worshipped Him, saying, my daughter IS EVEN NOW DEAD; but come and lay thy hand upon her, and SHE SHALL LIVE." Continuing in St Mark 5:35 to 43: (35) "While He yet spoke, there came from the ruler of the synagogue's house certain which said, thy daughter is dead: why trouble thou the Master any further? (36) As soon as Jesus heard the word that was spoken, He saith unto the ruler of the synagogue, be not afraid, ONLY BELIEVE. (37) Jesus suffered no man to follow Him,

save Peter, and James, and John the brother of James. (38) And He cometh to the house of the ruler of the synagogue, and sees the tumult, and them that wept and wailed greatly."

After they got to the house, Jesus said, do not weep for the damsel is asleep and not dead. They laughed at Jesus. Then Jesus took the father and mother plus the disciples that were with Him in where the daughter was. Then Jesus in verse: (41) "And He took the damsel by the hand, and said unto her, Talitha cumi; which is, being interpreted, 'damsel, I say unto thee, arise'. (42) And straightway the damsel arose and walked for she was of the age of twelve years. And they were astonished with a great astonishment. (43) And He charged them straightway, that no man should know it; and commanded that something should be given her to eat."

Then St Matthew 9:27-28-29: "And when Jesus departed thence, two blind men followed Him, crying, and saying, thou son of David, have mercy on us. (28) And when He was come into the house, the blind men came to Him: and Jesus said unto them, 'believe ye that I am able to do this?' They said unto Him, yea Lord. (29) Then touched He their eyes, saying, ACCORDING TO YOUR FAITH be it unto you."

They were healed, and their eyes were opened immediately. However, Jesus charged them not to tell anyone. Jesus told many people not to tell. Jesus knew when the word was spread about Him working, all these miracles, more of the priest and others would try and stop Jesus BEFORE His ministry was finished.

There are many other miracles recorded and not recorded. As St John says in 21:25:

"There are also many other things which Jesus did which, IF THEY SHOULD BE WRITTEN EVERYONE, I SUPPOSE THAT EVEN THE WORLD ITSELF COULD NOT CONTAIN THE BOOKS THAT SHOULD BE WRITTEN. Amen."

I said all of that to say this. Jesus would always find time to pray. A lot of times alone. Jesus was praying once, and His disciples came to Him. Jesus said, "who do the people say I am"? They answered and said, some say you are John the Baptist, or Elias or some prophet of old has risen again. Then Jesus said, "but who do you think I am". Peter said, "You are the Christ of God". Jesus then charged them to tell no man who He was.

Jesus then said Luke 9:22, "the Son of man must suffer many things, and be rejected of the elders and chief priests and scribes, and be slain, and be raised the third day". Jesus told His twelve disciples exactly what was going to happen, but they could not understand.

Then Jesus took Peter, John and James up in the mountain to pray.

Luke 9:29-30, "as He prayed the fashion of His countenance was altered. And His raiment was white and glistering. (30) And behold, there talked with Him two men, which were Moses and Elias".

They saw the two with Jesus, but they were heavy with sleep. When they awoke, Peter said it is good that we were here with you. Let us build three tabernacles. One for You and for Moses and for Elias. Peter knew who they were.

Luke 9:34-35, "While he was speaking there came a cloud, and overshadowed them; and they feared as they entered into the cloud. (35) And there came a voice out of the cloud, saying, 'this is my beloved Son: hear Him'."

Can you even feel a little of how Peter, John and James felt at that moment? I am setting here typing this and I cannot imagine how I would have felt while all of this was taking place. I LOVE you, Jesus. I cannot believe they would NOT have fallen on their face and worshipped God.

Jesus shared a lot with His disciples. He told them ALL the things that were going to happen to Him before they happened. They could not understand it at the time He told them. However, later they recalled what He had said.

Let me stop for a moment and say this. We do NOT know our future. How we will die. How long we will live. What will happen to us in the future? However, Jesus knew His future. He knew what was going to happen to Him, and even when it was going to happen. Jesus even told His disciples what was going to happen and when it was going to happen. They could NOT understand at that time.

Would you like to know your future? When you are going to die? How you are going to die? Where you are going to die? I first thought I would want to know, but we do not know the answer to any of these questions.

Jesus' disciples are some of the people that wrote the New Testament for us to read. After Peter, James and John wrote their books in the New Testament, they had to know for sure more than 1,000% that Jesus was the SON of GOD.

Read St Matthew 8:23 to 26. Jesus was in a boat with His disciples and He was asleep. A storm came and the boat was about to sink. They woke Jesus up and said we parish. Jesus told them, "O ye of little faith". Jesus stood up and rebuked the wind and there was a great calm.

St Matthews 8:27 "But the men marveled, saying; 'what manner of man is this, that even the winds and the sea obey Him'."

When they got to the other shore, they met two possessed with devils. Here we can see that even the devil knows that Jesus is the SON of GOD.

St Matthew 8:29, "And, behold, they cried out, saying; what have we to do with thee, Jesus, THOU SON OF GOD? Are thou come here to torment us before the time?"

Notice that even the devil BELIEVES that Jesus is the SON OF GOD, but you DO NOT see any devils in Heaven. Right?

We not only MUST believe Jesus is the Son of God, but we MUST accept Jesus as our personal Savior. A lot of people will say "I believe Jesus is the Son of God". However, you need to take the next step and accept Him as your personal Savior.

Sometimes life is about risking EVERYTHING you have and believing totally in Jesus Christ.

HOW MANY PEOPLE HAVE YOU SEEN WALKING ON WATER? HEALING "ALL" THE SICK THAT CAME TO HIM? RAISING THE DEAD?

Yes, I have seen many people healed with just the spoken word of God. I have not seen anyone walking on water. I have not seen anyone raising the dead. However, that does not mean I do not believe it. I DO believe it, with ALL my mind and heart. Jesus said we could do all of these.

St John 14:9, "Jesus said unto him, have I been so long time with you, and yet hast thou not known Me,

Philip? He that hath seen Me hast seen the Father; and how say thou then, show us the Father?"

Remember, me telling you that Jesus said, NO man has seen the Father at any time, but Jesus has revealed Him unto us?

I Timothy 2:5, "FOR THERE IS ONE GOD, and ONE MEDIATOR BETWEEN GOD and MEN, THE MAN CHRIST JESUS."

Hebrews 2:14-15, "Forasmuch then as the children are partakers of flesh and blood, He also Himself likewise took part of the same; that through death He might destroy him that had the power of death, that is, the devil. (15) And deliver them who through fear of death were all their lifetime subject to bondage."

St Luke 1:34-35, "Then said Mary unto the angel, 'how shall this be, seeing I know not a man?' (35) And the angel answered and said unto her, 'the Holy Spirit shall come upon thee, and the power of the Highest shall overshadow thee; therefore also that Holy Thing which shall be born of thee shall be called the SON OF GOD'."

<u>JUST A THOUGHT FOR YOU</u>. Mary, the mother of Jesus, KNEW Jesus was the SON OF GOD. I think as the mother of Jesus, she would have done ANYTHING to save Jesus' life—EXCEPT telling a lie. What if Mary tried to save Jesus from the cross, and she said, "JESUS CANNOT BE THE SON OF

GOD—HE IS THE SON OF JOSEPH"? They were crucifying Jesus because He said He was the SON OF GOD. Mary COULD NOT SAY HE IS NOT the SON OF GOD, because she KNEW THAT JESUS WAS THE SON OF GOD.

NO MATTER HOW LONG YOU HAVE TRAVELED IN THE WRONG DIRECTION, YOU CAN ALWAYS TURN AROUND.

Do you know that Jesus also sent groups of seventy out to tell the story of His Word? St Luke 10:1 to 5 also 9:

"(1) After these things, the Lord appointed ANOTHER seventy also, and, sent them two and two before His face into every city and place, whither He Himself would come. (2) Therefore, said He unto them, the harvest truly is great, but the laborers are few; pray ye therefore the Lord of the harvest, that He would send forth laborers unto His harvest. (3) Go your ways: behold, I send you forth as lambs among wolves. (4) Carry neither purse, nor scrip, nor shoes, and salute no man by the way. (5) And into whatsoever house ye enter; first say, peace be with you. (9) And heal the sick that are therein, and say unto them, the Kingdom of God is come nigh unto you."

Then in verse 17 same chapter says:

(17) "The seventy returned again with joy, saying, Lord, even the devils are subject to us through Your Name."

Jesus evidently did not minister as much after this until He returns to Jerusalem for the Jew's Passover.

As I have said before, I think St John had a uniquely special insight of Jesus. Please read St John 11:7 to 44. I will just write a few of the verses.

(7) "Then after that Jesus said to His disciples, 'let us go into Judea again'. (8) His disciples said unto Him, Master, the Jews of late sought to stone Thee, and You want to go there again?"

(14) "Then said Jesus unto them, 'Lazarus is dead. (15) And I am glad for your sakes that I was NOT there, to the intent ye may believe; nevertheless, let us go unto him'." Jesus said Lazarus WAS DEAD.

(21) "Then said Martha unto Jesus, if thou had been here, my brother would have not died. (22) But, I know, that EVEN NOW, whatsoever thou will ask of God, God will give it to thee".

(41) "Then they took away the stone from the place where Lazarus was dead. And Jesus lifted up His eyes, and said, Father, I thank Thee that Thou hast heard Me. (42) And I knew that Thou hear Me always, but because of the people which stand by I said it, that they may believe that Thou hast sent Me. (43) And when He

thus had spoken, He cried with a loud voice, 'Lazarus, come forth'. (44) And he that was dead came forth, bound hand and foot with graveclothes, and the face was bound about with a napkin. Jesus saith unto them, 'loose him, and let him go'."

Lazarus had two sisters—Martha and Mary. When Jesus' disciples warned Jesus not to go back to Judea, He wanted to go because of Lazarus' death. Also, to prove to His disciples and others that God had given Him power to raise the dead.

Before Jesus got to Lazarus' home, He stopped. Then Martha went to meet Jesus in verse 22, and that is when she said; "EVEN NOW God will do whatever you ask". Then Jesus said God will raise Lazarus up, she said; "I know He will at the end of time". She had just said; "EVEN NOW". She DID NOT believe what she had just said to Jesus.

Then Jesus sent for Mary. Mary left the house immediately and went to Jesus. She said the same thing that Martha said to Jesus. This is the Mary that is in St John 12:3 that put a pound of expensive ointment on the feet of Jesus then dried His feet with her hair. Of course, Judas Iscariot complained about it, and said they could have sold it to give to the poor.

Going back to verse 22 when Martha, said; "EVEN NOW". Think about that for a moment. They believed

Jesus could do ANYTHING, but, somehow, they did not believe Jesus would being Lazarus back from the dead. I think this is the way we are today. We KNOW Jesus can do ANYTHING, and sometimes we say; "EVEN NOW", but we do not believe it.

We know that was Jesus when God said, "let US make man in OUR image" in the first chapter of Genesis. Also, Jesus was referred to as WORD in the first chapter of St John when He helped God to create Adam. Why then, could Jesus not be able to bring Lazarus back to life?

I think in our present world, we feel Jesus can answer our prayers with small things and not ANYTHING. I thank God every day for the miracles that Jesus does in my life. I love you, Jesus.

Jesus knew all the time the priests and Pharisees were plotting to kill Him. Because of their plots against His life, Jesus walked no more openly among the Jews but withdrew briefly to Ephraim with His disciples (St John 11: 45 to 57).

Then six days before the Jewish Passover, Jesus went to Bethany where Lazarus and his family were.

Knowing that He could easily have stayed in relative safety in Ephraim, Jesus, nevertheless, chose to fulfill His mission of redemptive suffering. He returned to Jerusalem at Passover time for what was His final visit.

His triumphal entry was a public announcement of His messiahship St Matthew 21:1 to 11.

As Jesus was coming to Jerusalem, He stopped in Bethphage, near the Mount of Olives, before Jerusalem. There He asked two of His disciples to go and find a donkey and bring it back. Jesus said in verse two:

"(2) Go into the village over against you, and straightway ye shall find an ass tied, with a colt with her: loose them, and bring them to me. (3) And if any man say ought unto you, ye shall say. The Lord hath need of them. (4) All this was done, that it might be fulfilled which was spoken by the prophet, saying. (5) Tell ye the daughter of Sion, behold, the King cometh unto thee, meek, and sitting upon an ass, and a colt the foal of an ass. (8) And a very great multitude spread their garments in the way; others cut down branches from the trees, and strawed them in the way. (9) And the multitudes that went before, and that follow, cried, saying, Hosanna to the Son of David: Blessed is He that cometh in the name of the Lord; Hosanna in the highest."

Think about this for a moment. When Jesus came into Jerusalem for the Passover, the people were shouting His name to the Lord. They were putting their clothes and branches from trees for Him to travel on. Then in just a few days some of them would be crying "crucify Him". How can that be? All of this had to take place to fulfill the words of the prophet in the Old Testament.

Zachariah told about this happening 487 years before the birth of our Lord (Jesus). Zechariah 9:9 says:

"Rejoice greatly, O daughter of Zion; shout, O daughter of Jerusalem: behold, thy King cometh unto thee. He is just, and having salvation; lowly, and riding upon an ass, and upon a colt the foal of an ass."

St Luke 19:38 to 41 reads like this:

"Blessed be the King that cometh in the name of the Lord: peace in Heaven, and glory in the highest. (39) And some of the Pharisees from among the multitude said unto Him, rebuke thy disciples. (40) And He answered and said unto them, 'I tell you that, if these should hold their peace, the stones would immediately cry out'. (41) And when He was come near, He beheld the city, and wept over it."

Jesus announced the future destruction of Jerusalem (St Luke 19:42 to 44). That is the reason, when He saw Jerusalem, He wept. All the people could not understand what Jesus was saying, but Jesus knew. Yes, Jerusalem was completely, destroyed in 70 AD. That was 37 years after the death of Jesus. According to prophecies, it was because Jerusalem had turned their face from God. Also, they were going to crucify Jesus, and He knew it.

Then Jesus went in the Temple in St Luke 19:45 and 46:

"And He went in the Temple, and began to cast out them that sold therein, and them that bought; (46) Saying unto them, it is written, My house is the house of prayer: but ye have made it a den of thieves."

Then Jesus taught in the Temple and preached the gospel. The chief priest, scribes and elders came to Jesus and asked; tell us by what authority do you teach? Jesus answered, and, said; "I will answer you if you answer my question. Was John the Baptist's ministry from Heaven or man?"

The priest, scribes and elders knew the people loved John the Baptist. So, they said amount themselves, If, we say from Heaven, then Jesus will say, why did you not believe him? If we say from man, the people will want to stone us. The people thought John the Baptist was a prophet. They answered we cannot tell which one it was. Then Jesus said unto them; "Neither tell I by what authority I do these things."

Then Jesus spoke a parable to them and the people; St Luke 20:9 to 16:

(9) "A certain Man planted a vineyard, and let it forth husbandmen, and went into a far country for a long time. (10) And all the season He sent a servant to the husbandmen, that they should give Him of the fruit of the vineyard: but the husbandmen beat him and sent him away empty. (11) And, again, He sent

another servant; and they beat him also, and entreated him shamefully, and sent him away. (12) And, again, He sent a third: and they wounded him, also, and cast him out. (13) Then said the LORD of the vineyard, what shall I do? I will send My BELOVED SON: it, may be, they will reverence HIM when they see HIM. (14) And when the husbandmen saw Him, they reasoned among themselves, saying, this is the heir: come let us kill Him, that the inheritance may be ours. (15) So, they cast Him out of the vineyard, and killed Him. What therefore shall the LORD of the vineyard do unto them? (16) He shall come and destroy these husbandmen and shall give the vineyard to others. And when they heard it, they said, God forbid".

Can you NOT see that Jesus was talking about God, the Father as "LORD" OF THE VINEYARD, and Jesus, "MY BELOVED SON" in this parable? Like the parable says, God is going to destroy the people that destroyed His Son. The chief priests and scribes were to blind to see what Jesus was saying in the parable, and they said, "God forbid".

Then the chief priests and scribes tried to get ANYTHING they could against Jesus so they could put Him to death. They even sent spies in where Jesus was teaching to try and find something that He might say to use against Jesus.

In my opinion, the chief priests and scribes were controlled by the devil at this point.

They asked Jesus; is it lawful to give tribute unto Caesar or not? Jesus said in; St Luke 20:23 to 25:

"Why do you temp me? (24) Show me a penny. Whose image is on it? They answered and said Caesar. (25) Then Jesus said, render unto Caesar what is Caesar's and unto God what is God's."

After asking Jesus a couple more questions, which Jesus answered, then the chief priests and scribes stopped asking Jesus any more questions. Nevertheless, Jesus kept teaching the people in the Temple by day, and at night He would go to a place called the Mount of Olives.

Now the feast of the unleavened bread which is called the Passover was drawing near. So, the priests and scribes had to find a way to destroy Jesus. Then entered satan into Judas Iscariot which is one of the twelve. He went to the chief priests and captains to asked how he might betray Jesus? They offered him 40 pieces of silver to help them when the multitudes were not around. Judas told them where Jesus prayed and spent His time at night.

Then Jesus sent Peter and John into the city to secure the upper room for Jesus and the twelve to have Jesus' Last Supper. There Jesus said, St Matthew 26:21 to 25:

(21) "And as they did eat, He said, verily I say unto you, that one of you shall betray Me. (22) And they

were exceeding sorrowful, and began every one of them to say unto Him, Lord, is it I? (23) And He answered and said, he that dips his hand with Me in the dish, the same shall betray Me. (24) The Son of man goes as it is written of him: but woe unto that man by whom the Son of man is betrayed! It had been good for that man if he had not been born. (25) Then Judas, which betrayed Him, answered and said, Master, is it I? He said unto him, thou hast said."

Jesus already knew it was Judas that was going to betray Him. Jesus and Judas dipped their hand in the dish at the same time.

Then continuing in verse 26 to 34:

(26) "And as they were eating, Jesus took bread, and blessed it, and brake it, and gave it to the disciples, and said, take, eat; this is my body. (27) And He took the cup, and gave thanks, and gave it to them, saying drink ye all of it. (28) For this is My blood of the new testament, which is shed for many for the remission of sins. (29) But I say unto you, I will not drink henceforth of this fruit of the vine, until that day when I drink it new (with you) in My Father's Kingdom. (30) And when they had sung a hymn, they went out unto the Mount of Olives. (31) Then said Jesus unto them, all of you shall be offended because of me this night; for it is written, I will smite the Shepard, and the sheep of the flock shall be scattered abroad. (32) But after I am risen again, I will

go before you into Galilee. (33) Peter answered and said unto Him, though all men shall be offended because of thee, yet will I never be offended. (34) Jesus said unto him, verily I say unto you, that this night, before the rooster crows, you shall deny me three times."

At least we know that Peter followed to see what they were doing to Jesus. All the others were hiding behind closed doors.

Let me stop and point out something very, special when Moses did the Passover with the children of Israel Exodus 12:7-8 and 11: "They shall take of the blood (from the lamb), and strike it on the two side posts and on the upper door post of the houses, wherein they shall EAT IT (the lamb). (8) And they shall EAT the flesh in that night, with fire, and unleavened bread; and with bitter herbs they shall EAT IT. (11) And thus, SHALL YE EAT IT (THE LAMB); with your loins girded, your shoes on your feet, and your staff in your hand; and ye SHALL EAT in the haste; IT IS THE LORD'S PASSOVER."

When Jesus had the Passover with the twelve disciples, there is no place it says they ate of a LAMB. The reason was the LAMB was SETTING at the table with them. All they had was bread and wine. The reason was JESUS WAS THE LAMB. When they ATE the BREAD, "JESUS said THIS IS MY BODY (LAMB)". JESUS WAS THE ONLY LAMB

WITHOUT BLEMISH. Remember, when John the Baptist saw Jesus coming to him to be baptized; he said, "behold the LAMB OF GOD"?

After Jesus' last supper, He and His disciples went to a place called Gethsemane. Then He said stay here, while I go yonder and pray. Jesus took Peter, John and James with Him. He told them to watch and pray. Then He fell on His knees and prayed. He asked God if it were possible to keep Him from having to go through all the things to come. However, not my will, but My Father, God's will be done. Jesus goes to the three disciples that were with Him, and they were asleep. Jesus said you can not watch and pray for one hour? Jesus goes back to pray again. This time St Luke 22:44 describes it like this:

"And being in an agony He prayed more earnestly; and His sweat was as it were great DROPES OF BLOOD falling down to the ground."

This time when He goes back to the three disciples, He said My hour is here. Then the four of them go to meet the other disciples. That is when Judas and the mob show up to take Jesus.

Peter pulls his sword and cuts off the right ear of the servant of the high priest. Jesus told him to put his sword away. Then Jesus touches the servant's ear and healed him.

Jesus said to the mob; you saw me daily in the Temple, yet you come in the night to arrest me? The mob took Jesus away.

They did not arrest Him in the Temple because the people loved Him. They were afraid of what the people would do.

I know you have heard the story before, but I need to repeat it again. Jesus goes through all these things for MY sins and sickness, and for YOUR sins and sickness.

Jesus was beaten, laughed at, spit upon, made fun of, mocked, forsaken and every other thing that you could imagine. They blindfolded Him then struck Him on the face and asked Him to prophesy "who is it that smote you?" Then they hung Him on a cross, the most shameful and worst punishment a human can go through.

Just STOP for a moment and think of all the things that Jesus went through for you and me. All of this so we can be forgiven of OUR sins (NOT HIS) and be healed. I WANT YOUR HEART TO ACHE. I WANT YOUR MIND TO TELL YOU TO STOP AND THINK ABOUT WHAT JESUS DID FOR YOU AND ME. NOT BECAUSE HE SINNED, BUT BECAUSE WE SINNED. GOD HELP US.

The priest and mob took Jesus to Pilate. Pilate said, "I find no fault in this man". Pilate did not want to deal with Jesus, so he sent Him to Herod. Then Herod sent Jesus back to Pilate to deal with Him. Pilate still found no fault in him. The priest said Jesus is teaching things that are not true. They hated it when Jesus would tell them He is the Son of God.

According to their tradition they would release one prisoner before the Passover. So, Pilate decided to wash his hands of Jesus and see what the people wanted; Jesus or Barabbas to be released. Barabbas was in jail for murder. Pilate still willing to release Jesus, said what do you want me to do with Jesus? Pilate still willing to release Jesus said, what do you want me to do with Jesus? Pilate knew Jesus was innocent. The crowd cried, "CRUCIFY HIM, CRUCIFY HIM". Then Pilate said in St Luke 23:22 to 25:

(22) "And he said unto them the third time, why, what evil hath He done? I have found no cause for death in Him; I will, therefore, chastise Him, and let Him go. (23) And they were instant with loud voices, requiring that He might be CRUCIFIED. And the voices of them and of the CHIEF PRIEST prevailed. (24) And Pilate gave sentence that it should be as they required. (25) And he released unto them him that for sedition and murder was cast into prison, whom they desired; but he delivered Jesus to their will."

THINK FOR A MOMENT... Jesus was a threat to the priests and scribes, so they wanted Jesus dead.

I do not know who to blame for the death of Jesus. However, I can see that ALL of them went along with it. Pilate was willing to let Jesus go. Some in the crowd and PRIEST and SCRIBES cried out "CRUCIFY HIM". We know the priest wanted Him dead. The devil wanted Jesus dead. MAYBE WE SHOULD NOT WANT TO PLACE BLAME, BUT JUST SAY THIS IS A PROPHESY THAT WAS FULFILLED AND IT WAS COMPLETED.

After Jesus was beaten and tortured until He did not even look like a human, they tried to get Him to carry His cross to a place called Calvary. He was to weak to carry it, all the way, so they got a man called Simon to help Jesus carry His cross. You need to know that history tells us that Simon was a black man. GREAT for the black people. I KNOW God blessed him for helping Jesus' carry His cross.

As I am writing this at 1:30 AM and my eyes are filled with tears. Who could ever believe that someone would LOVE us enough to go through ALL of this? Sorry, but I must stop for now and pray and thank Jesus for doing all of this for us. In all the days of my long life, I have never felt this close to Christ Jesus.

Maybe I can continue writing now.

St Luke 23:27-28 "And there followed Him a great company of people, and of women, which also bewailed and lamented Him. (28) But Jesus turning unto them said, 'daughters of Jerusalem, weep not for Me, but weep for yourselves, and for your children'." He took time to prophesy of the destruction of Jerusalem in 70 A D. This tells us that Jesus was a SUPER NATIONAL HUMAN to know all the things that are going to take place in the future.

St Mark 15:29 to 34 and 37 describes what it was like while Jesus was on the cross:

(29) "And they that passed by railing on Him, wagging their hands, and saying, You, that destroys the Temple, and builds it back in three days. (30) Save thyself, and, come down from the cross. (31) Likewise, also the CHIEF PRIEST mocking said among themselves with the SCRIBES, He saved others; himself He cannot save. (32) Let Christ the King of Israel descend now from the cross, that we may see and believe. And they that were crucified with Him reviled Him. (33) And when the sixth hour was come, there was darkness over the whole land until the ninth hour. (34) And the ninth hour Jesus cried with a loud voice, saying, E-lo-i, E-lo-I, la-masa-bach-tha-ni? Which is being interpreted, My God, My God, why hast thou forsaken Me?"

In verse (37) "Jesus cried with a loud voice and gave up the Ghost." He died.

Let me make SURE you understand three things here. When Jesus said He would destroy this Temple and in three days rebuild it. Jesus was talking about HIS BODY. Jesus died, and after three days He rose (rebuilt) from the dead. Second thing to clarify is the priest told Jesus to come down from the cross and they would believe Him. We KNOW that is NOT true. They knew Jesus had power over death. He raised Lazarus from the dead only days before this. And third Jesus cried and said God had FORSAKEN Him. God CANNOT look upon SIN. JESUS TOOK <u>ALL</u> THE SINS OF THE WORLD UPON HIMSELF ON THE CROSS. THAT IS THE REASON GOD TURNED HIS FACE FROM JESUS. GOD WOULD "NEVER" FORSAKE JESUS.

St Luke 23:35 to 37 and 42 to 45 tells us of the things taking place during the crucifixion. There were two men crucified with Jesus--one on the left and one on the right. Jesus looked over the crowd of priests, soldiers and people and, said, "Father, forgive them; for they know not what they do". Can you picture this? After they had just beaten, tortured, mocked and all the other things to Jesus, He looks over the crowd of priest, soldiers and people and said, "Father forgive them, for they know not what they do". Sorry, but it is hard for me to see that MUCH LOVE IN ONE PERSON.

(35) "And the people stood beholding, and the rulers also with them derided Him, saying, He saved others; let Him save Himself, if He be Christ, the chosen of God. (36) And the soldiers also mocked Him, coming to Him, and offering Him vinegar. (37) Saying, if thou be the king of the Jews, save Thyself."

There was a sign written in Greek, Latin and Hebrew and placed over the head of Jesus saying; "This is the King of the Jews".

One man hanging next to Jesus said, "if thou be Christ, save thyself and save us." And the other man told him to be silent. He said we deserve to be here, but Jesus does not. Then he said in verse (42) "And he said unto Jesus, remember me when thou come into thy Kingdom. (43) And Jesus said unto him, verily I say unto thee, to day shalt thou be with Me in Paradise. (44) And it was about the sixth hour, and there was a darkness over all the earth until the ninth hour. (45) And the sun was darkened, and the veil of the Temple was rent in the midst."

Now let us pick this up in the book of St Matthew as how he described what happened during the crucifixion Matthew 27:50 to 54 and 59 to 63 and 66:

(50) "Jesus, when He had cried again with a loud voice, yielded up the ghost. (51) And behold, the veil of the temple was rent in twain from the top to the bottom;

and the earth did quake, and the rocks rent. (52) And the graves were opened; and many bodies of the saints which slept arose. (53) And came out of the graves after His resurrection, and went into the holy city, and appeared unto many. (54) Now when the centurion, and they that were with him, watching Jesus, saw the earthquake, and those things that were done, they feared greatly, saying, 'Truly this was the SON of GOD'."

Joseph asked Pilate if he could take Jesus' body, and he said yes. (59) "And when Joseph (of Arimathaea) and Nicodemus had taken the Body, he wrapped It in a clean linen cloth. (60) And laid It in his own new tomb, which he had hewn out of a rock; and he ROLLED a GREAT STONE TO THE DOOR of the tomb and departed."

(62) "NOW THE NEXT DAY, that followed the day of the preparation, the chief priests and Pharisees came together unto Pilate. (63) Saying Sir, we remember that the Deceiver said, while He was yet alive. After three days I will rise again."

(66) "So, they went, and made the tomb sure, sealing the stone, and setting a watch."

Put soldiers in front of the tomb to watch WITH A LARGE/GREAT STONE COVERING THE DOOR. Then after three days: Matthew 28:2,3,4

(2) "And behold, there was a great earthquake; for the angel of the Lord descended from Heaven, and,

came and rolled back the stone from the door and sat upon it. (3) His countenance was like lightning, and his raiment white as snow. (4) And for fear of him the keepers (soldiers) did shake and became as dead men."

Then the soldiers went to the elders and chief priests and told them what had happened. The chief priest and elders offered the soldiers a large sum of money to say; "His disciples came by night and stole Him away while we slept". These soldiers had to be very SOUND sleepers to not know someone came and ROLLED the LARGE/GREAT STONE AWAY WITHOUT WAKING THEM UP. The soldiers took the money and told everyone this story. Even to this day, this story is reported among some of the Jews.

In St Mark 16:1 TO 4:

"And when the Sabbath was past, Mary Magdalene, and Mary the mother of James, and Salome, had brought sweet spices, that they might come and anoint Him. (2) And very, early in the morning the first day of the week, they came unto the sepulchre at the rising of the sun. (3) And they said among themselves, WHO SHALL ROLL us AWAY the STONE FROM the DOOR of the tomb? (4) And when they looked, they saw that the stone was rolled away: FOR IT WAS VERY GREAT."

Mark 16:1; Mary Magdalene, from the village of Magdala along the sea of Galilee, who Jesus healed her of seven demons came to the tomb and was one of the first to know of the resurrection.

Also, Mary the mother of James and Joses was one of the women who joined Jesus' party in His tours of Galilee and provided Him with food and money.

Also, Salome one of the group of women who followed Jesus. This Salome was from Galilee, and the wife of Zebedee (a successful fisherman on the sea of Galilee) and the mother of James and John, two of the twelve disciples.

I just wanted to clarify this a little because there were many Mary's and John's in the life of Jesus.

Mary, mother of John Mark, this Mary was a well-to-do woman in Jerusalem who became one of the earlier followers of Jesus. Her house became the unofficial meeting place for the earliest band of believers after the resurrection, and probably the location of the "Upper Room". The disciples congregated there after the crucifixion and resurrection, praying together at the time of Pentecost. They were praying there when James was put to death and Peter imprisoned. She was related to one of the leaders of the church of Antioch. Tradition claims that Mary's house was not destroyed when Titus took Jerusalem in 70 A D but was used as a church in later years (Acts 12:12).

I must ask again. How did the soldiers sleep while someone came and stole the body of Jesus from the tomb? You must believe, what the Bible said, an angel appeared in white, bright light and the soldiers became AS DEAD men. The soldiers knew what happened and told the priest. The priest paid the soldiers money to LIE. The soldiers then LIED to the people (Matthew 28:11 to 15).

After Mary Magdalene, Mary the mother of James and Salome had reached the tomb. The stone was rolled away. They looked inside and saw a young man and were frighten St Mark 16:5 to 8:

(5) "Entering into the sepulchre, they saw a young man sitting on the right side, clothed in a long white garment; and they were affrighted. (6) And he said unto them, be not affrighted: ye seek Jesus of Nazareth, which was crucified: He is risen; He is not here: behold the place where they laid Him. (7) But go your way, tell His disciples and Peter that He goes before you into Galilee: there shall ye see Him, as He said unto you. (8) And they went out quickly and fled from the sepulchre; for they trembled and were amazed: neither said they anything to any man; for they were afraid."

Then in verses 9. 10 and 11 St Mark 16: tells us that Mary Magdalene was the first one to see Jesus after He was risen. She goes back to the disciples and told them, and they did not believe her.

St Mark 16:12 and 14:

"After that He appeared in another form unto two of them, as they walked, and went into the country. (14) Afterward He appeared unto the eleven as they sat at meat and upbraided them with their unbelief and hardness of heart, because they believed not them which had seen Him after He was risen."

I have told you what Matthew, Mark and Luke had to say about the crucifixion, now I would like to tell you a little about what St John says. His writings are some of the best in the new Testament. Jesus was praying in Gethsemane and the mob with Judas came to arrest Jesus. Jesus said, "whom do you seek?" They said Jesus of Nazareth. Jesus said, "I am He", and only in St John it says, "they went backward, and fell to the ground". It must have been the power of God. Jesus asked them again, "whom do you seek?" They said Jesus. You know the story of Simon Peter drawing his sword and cutting the high priest servant's ear off, and Jesus healing him. The servant's name was Malchus. Jesus told Peter to put his sword away.

St John 18:12 to 14 says:

(12) "Then the band and the captain and OFFICERS OF THE JEWS took Jesus and bound Him. (13) And led Him away to Annas first: for he was father-in-law to Calaphas, which was the high priest that same year."

Calaphas counsel the Jews that it was better, that just one man to die for the people. Now they had Jesus, they did not know what to do with Him, so they took Him to Annas' house.

Peter and Judas followed the mob to Pilate. The priest knew Judas. Then Judas asked, if Peter could come in the gate. There was a damsel that kept the door. Then, the damsel asked Peter, "are you not one of the disciples?" Peter said I am not. That was the first time Peter denied Jesus. Then Peter stood by the fire with the servants and officers because it was very cold. Then one that stood by the fire asked Peter (second time) if he were one of the disciples? Peter said I am not.

Then one of the servants of the high priest, that was kin to the one that Peter cut off his ear, asked Peter (third time), are you not one of the disciples? Peter said I am not, and immediately the rooster crowed. Jesus told Peter this would happen.

After taking Jesus to Pilate. St John 18:29 to 31 and 36-37:

(29) "Pilate then went out unto them, and said, 'what accusation bring ye against this Man'? (30) They answered and said unto him, if He were not a malefactor, we would not have delivered Him unto you. (31) Then said Pilate unto them, take ye Him, and judge Him according to your law. THE JEWS therefore said unto

him, it is NOT LAWFUL FOR US TO PUT ANY MAN TO DEATH."

Pilate asked Jesus again, "are you the King of the Jews?" Pilate told Jesus your OWN NATION and the CHIEF PRIEST have delivered you unto me. What have You done?

(36) "Jesus, answered; My kingdom is not of this world: if My kingdom were of this world, then would My servants fight, that I should not be delivered to THE JEWS: but now is My kingdom not from here. (37) Pilate therefore said unto Him, 'art Thou a King'? Jesus answered, thou sayest that I am a King. To this end was I born, and for this cause came I unto the world, that I should bear witness unto the truth. Every one that is of the truth hearth My voice. (38) Pilate said unto Him, 'what is truth'?"

Pilate then goes back to THE JEWS and said I find no fault in this Man. Then he said you have a custom that I release one unto you for the Passover. Do you want me to release unto you the King of the Jews, or Barabbas a murder? Then Pilate scourged Jesus and the soldiers platted a crown of thorns on His head and put a purple robe on Him. St John 19:3-4:

(3) "And said, Hail, King of the Jews, and they smote Him with their hands." (4) Pilate therefore went forth

again, and said unto them, behold, I bring Him forth to you, that you may know that I find no fault in Him."

When the CHIEF PRIEST and OFFICERS saw Him, THEY CRIED OUT, CRUCIFY HIM, CRUCIFY HIM. Pilate said take ye Him and crucify Him, but I find no fault in Him. The Jews said unto Pilate, we have a law that Jesus should die because He made Himself the "Son of God". When Pilate heard them say that, he was more afraid. So, he takes Jesus back in the judgement hall and asked, "where are You from?" However, Jesus answered not a word. Pilate said, why do You not say a word? Do You not know I have the power to crucify you, or release You? St John 19:11, 12:

(11) "Jesus answered, Thou, could have no power at all against Me, except it were given you from above: therefore, he that delivered Me unto you hath the greater sin. (12) And from thenceforth Pilate sought to release Him: but the JEWS cried out, saying, if you let this Man go, you are not Caesar's friend: whosoever makes Himself king speaks against Caesar."

When Pilate hear this, he really did not know what to do. In verse 14 Pilate brought Jesus out in front of the JEWS and said. "behold your King". But they cried out, away with Him, crucify Him. Pilate said in verse 15, do you want me to crucify your King? Then the CHIEF PRIEST said, we have no king but Caesar. Then Pilate released Jesus to them to be crucified. They lead Him with His cross to a place, in Hebrew, called Golgotha.

St John 19:23 & 24 After Jesus was crucified the soldiers tore His garment in four pieces one for each soldier. However, the coat was without seam, woven from the top throughout. Let us cast lots for it and have one winner. All of this was done so the scriptures could be fulfilled. Written hundreds of years before: in Psalms 22:18 by King David, "they parted My garment among them, and for My vesture they did cast lots". These things therefore the soldiers did.

Standing at the foot of the cross was Jesus' mother, her sister, Mary wife of Cleophas and Mary Magdalene. Looking down He saw His mother and His beloved disciple. Then said Jesus to His beloved disciple, "behold thy mother; and from that hour that disciple took Mary into his own home".

The JEWS did not want Jesus hanging on the cross after 6 PM, because it would go into one of their three sabbath days that week. They asked Pilate to brake Jesus' legs to make sure He was dead so Jesus could be taken off the cross. The soldiers came to break their legs. The legs of the two (one on the right and one on the left) they broke, but when they came to Jesus; He was already dead. So, the soldier took a spear and pushed into the side of Jesus and out came blood and water. YES, JESUS WAS DEAD! JESUS SHED ALL HIS BLOOD FOR

YOU AND FOR ME. All of us know the body cannot live without blood in it. YES, JESUS WAS DEAD.

These things were done like this so a prophesy shall be fulfilled, "a bone of Jesus shall not be broken". It was written 1490 years before the birth of Christ. Written by Moses in the book of Numbers 9:12; "They shall leave none of it before morning, nor break ANY bone of it: according to all the ordinances of the Passover they shall keep."

Then Joseph of Arimathaea being a disciple of Jesus, but secretly for fear of the Jews. He asked Pilate if he could take the body of Jesus. Pilate said okay. Joseph and Nicodemus took Jesus' body to a sepulchre in a garden near where He was crucified and wherein was NEVER a man yet laid. Nicodemus brought a hundred-pound mixture of myrrh and aloes. They wrapped the body in linen clothes with spices as the manner of the Jews is to bury. St John 19:42: "There laid they Jesus therefore because of the Jews preparation day; for the sepulchre was nigh at hand."

St John 20:1: "The first day of the week cometh Mary Magdalene early, when it was yet dark, unto the sepulchre. She saw the stone had been taken away from the sepulchre."

She ran to tell Simon Peter and the other disciples that someone has taken our Lord away. So, Peter and another disciple (I would guess this was John) ran to the tomb to see. They looked inside to see the linen clothes were lying there. The napkin that was covering the face and head was with the linen but wrapped together in a place by itself. Both disciples went inside and saw the linen. At this point they did not know the scriptures that He must rise again from the dead. Even though Jesus had told them just days before this. Everyone was confused and did not know what to do. Jesus had told them exactly what was going to happen. Now it was all playing out the way Jesus said. These disciples returned to their own home.

Mary Magdalene did not leave but stood outside the tomb and swept. As she was weeping, she looked inside the tomb and saw two angels in white. One setting at the head and one setting at the feet of where the body of Jesus was. The two angels said, woman why do you weep? She said unto them because they have taken my Lord away, and I know not where they have laid Him. Then she turned around and saw Jesus and did not know it was Him. St John 20:15 to 20:

"Jesus said unto her, woman, why do you weep? Who sleekest thou? She, supposing Him to be the gardener, said unto Him, Sir, if thou have borne, Him hence, tell me where thou hath laid Him, and I will take Him away. (16) Jesus said unto her, Mary, she turned herself, and said unto Him, Rabboni; which is to say, Master.

(17) Jesus said unto her, 'touch Me not; for I AM NOT YET ASCENDED TO MY FATHER: but go to My brethren, and say unto them, I ascend unto My Father, and your Father; and to My God, and your God. (18) Mary Magdalene came and told the disciples that she had seen the Lord, and that He had spoken these things unto her. (19) Then the same day at evening, being the first day of the week, when the doors were shut where the disciples were assembled for fear of the Jews, came Jesus and stood in the midst, and said unto them, 'peace be unto you'. (20) And when He so said, He showed unto them His hands and His side. Then were the disciples glad, when, they saw the Lord."

They STILL needed that proof of Jesus showing them His hands and His side. Did you notice that the disciples were assembled and shut up with locked doors and Jesus appeared unto them? They could touch Him and see He was not a Ghost. Jesus had a Heavenly Body. He came through the door/wall whatever but still they could touch Him. Glory be to God. When we get to Heaven, what kind of a body will we have? Notice Jesus said in verse 17 He was going to ascend to His Father AND, our Father, to His God AND, our God? God belong to US ALSO.

Thomas called Didymus, one of the twelve was not with the disciples when Jesus appeared to them. The others told him about seeing Jesus, "but he said unto them. Except I shall see in His hands the print of the nails, and thrust my hand into His side, I WILL NOT BELIEVE." Jesus had His Heavenly body with scars to prove who He was.

Then after eight days the disciples were locked in the room, and Jesus APPEARED unto them. And again, He said unto them, "peace be unto you" Then St John 20:27 to 29:

(27) "Then said He to Thomas, 'reach hither thy finger, and behold my hands; and reach hither thy hand, and thrust it unto my side: and be not faithless, but believing. (28) And Thomas answered and said unto Him, my LORD and my GOD. (29) Jesus saith unto him, Thomas, because thou hast seen Me, thou hast believed: <u>BLESSED ARE THEY THAT HAVE NOT SEEN, AND YET HAVE BELIEVED</u>."

St John goes on in verses 30 and 31 to say there were many other signs that Jesus did in the present of His disciples that are NOT written in this book. The above things are written that we might believe that Jesus is the Christ, the Son of God; and that BELIEVING WE MIGHT HAVE "LIFE" THROUGH HIS NAME.

That is ALL of us. We have NOT seen yet we believe. I hope ALL of you reading this book can believe. Jesus and God are real.

This is a TRUE story. This story is NOT fiction. This really took place. There are witnesses that were there. You can choose to believe it or dismiss it as a fairy tale. I choose to believe it. It is ALL REAL. It is God telling ALL of us, even 2000 years after, all, of these things took place.

If only I could be with you there, while reading this book...

After Jesus rose from the dead, He said to His disciples in St Matthew 28:19 and 20.

"Go ye therefore, and teach all nations, baptizing them in the name of the Father, and of the Son, and of the Holy Spirit. (20) Teaching them to observe all things whatsoever I have commended you: and lo, I AM WITH YOU ALWAYS, even unto the end of the world. Amen."

Some of the gospels tell the same story, they just tell it in a little different way.

Get ready for ABUNDANCE. Peter caught SO MANY fishes until his net was breaking-- ABUNDANCE. Jesus feed the multitude with FIVE loafs of bread and TWO fishes, and all of them were filled. Then His disciples collected TWELVE baskets that were left over—ABUNDANCE. There was a lot more left over after the multitude had eaten and was full, than they had before with the five loafs of bread and two fishes—ABUNDANCE.

I have fished a lot in my life. Therefore, I need to tell you something. When you say FISH, that can mean one FISH or a thousand FISH of the same kind of fish. However, when you say FISHES, that means different kind of fish. The same kind of fish run together (in what is called schools of fish) in the water. Peter caught FISHES. That means different kind of fish. God had to get different kind of fish to swim to gather for Peter to catch FISHES.

David said my cup is running OVER. David did not say my cup is full. He said my cup runs over. Expect ABUNDANCE.

I am getting ready to talk about Jesus being like God. However, before I do, maybe we should transition from Jesus being a man here on earth to a Heavenly body. Yes, I said a HEAVENLY BODY, one like God.

After Jesus rising from the dead on the third day, Mary Magdalene was the first one to see Jesus alive—HEAVENLY BODY. Then the same day, in the evening, Jesus appeared unto His disciples in a closed room. It was the first day of the week. We have talked about Jesus going through the wall or door when it was locked—HEAVENLY BODY. Then Jesus showed His disciples (Thomas not present) His hands and His side, and they were glad it was the Lord—HEAVENLY BODY.

Remember Thomas (a disciple) said he would not believe until he touched Jesus' hand, and pushed into Jesus' side. Later he got to touch Jesus'—HEAVENLY BODY.

Do you recall us talking about Jesus appearing to about seven of His disciples on the sea of Tiberias. After fishing all night, Jesus asked them if they had any meat. They said they had not caught anything. Jesus told them to cast their net on the right side, and they caught so many fishes till the net was about to break. Then they recognized it was the Lord. Jesus already had a fire burning. Then Jesus took some bread and fish, and they did eat—HEAVENLY BODY. This was the third time Jesus had shown Himself to His disciples.

Recap a few of the things with our HEAVENLY BODY. Jesus went through a wall or locked door but still had a HEAVENLY BODY that you could TOUCH. Jesus eat food with His HEAVENLY BODY. A lot of this can be found in St John chapters 20 and 21.

How do I feel? I feel there will be no LIMITATION to us with our HEAVENLY BODY. Of course, all of that is within God's will. Stop and think about this for a moment. We will never be sick. We will never grow old. We will love everyone, and they will love us. We will be joyful all the time. We will have peace all the time. MOST OF ALL WE WILL BE WITH JESUS. I am looking forward to getting my HEAVENLY BODY!!!!!!!

ONE MORE THOUGHT about the HEAVENLY BODY. What if Jesus had gone to the disciples with a HEAVENLY BODY WITHOUT SCARS? Then the disciples would have said THIS IS AN ANGEL and NOT JESUS. Sometimes we must live with our scars and be proud of them.

PS: Before we move on to the last chapter, I need to talk a little more about the apostle that Jesus loved very much. I told you before that John, the apostle, was my favorite person in the New Testament. He was the son of Zebedee and the brother of James the apostle. John and James ran a fishing business in Capernaum. He was called by His cousin Jesus to become, one of the twelve, and was always included as one of the inner circles among the disciples. John, with Peter and James, were the ones selected to be with Jesus at the raising of Jairus' daughter from the dead, also the transfiguration, and at Gethsemane. John and Peter were selected to prepare the Last Supper. John was the one at the foot of the cross Jesus entrusted His mother, Mary, to live with his family. John's ambitious mother tried to get places of prominence for John and James in Jesus' Kingdom. When the first report of the resurrection reached the disciples, John was the first to race to the empty tomb. He was looked up to, as one of the leaders among Jesus' followers. He was arrested after healing and preaching boldly before the authorities. Paul refers to John with respect. John's reverent, eye-witness account of Jesus' life make him one of the greatest literary of history. He wrote at least five books in the Bible, and that includes the book of Revelation written in 96 AD. He wrote the Gospel According to St John in 85 to 90 AD and also 1st, 2nd and 3rd John in 90 AD. John is the only one of the twelve that was not put to death by Jesus' enemies. History say John died of old age in exile on Patmos. But wait, Jesus had just told Peter how and when he was going to die (St John 21:18-19). Then Peter saw John, whom Jesus loved, which also leaned on Jesus' breast at the Last Supper. St John 21:21-23:

"Peter seeing him saith to Jesus, Lord and what shall this man (John) do? (22) Jesus saith unto him (Peter), if I will that he (John) tarry until I come, what is that to thee? Follow thou Me. (23) Then went this saying abroad among the brethren, that John should not die: yet Jesus said not to him, he shall not die; but, if I will that he should tarry till I come, what is that to thee (Peter)?"

So, Jesus did not tell Peter that John was not going to die, but if Jesus wanted John to live until Jesus returned, what is that to Peter? How would you INTERPRET verse 22? Again, history tells us that John died of old age on the island of Patmos.

Jesus really blessed John to write the book of Revelation and to inspire all of the Lord's followers.

JUST ANOTHER THOUGHT FOR YOU

How many times in the Bible was Jesus referred to as the LAMB of God? Hundreds of times, but Jesus was NOT sacrificed like all the other LAMBS had been. All the LAMBS sacrificed in the Bible had their throat cut AND they died in a few seconds. However, Jesus DID NOT die like that. He was TORTURED for an entire night and part of the morning. Then He was TORTURED for over six hours hanging on a cross before He died. THAT IS "NOT" WHAT ALL THE OTHER "LAMBS" WENT THROUGH BEFORE THEY DIED. YES, He was sacrificed for ALL of us. YES, He died for ALL of us. YES, He was the "LAMB OF GOD". However, He was NOT treated like ALL the other sacrificed LAMBS FOR GOD. JUST THINK ABOUT THAT.

Was Jesus like God?

Now for the third question. Is Jesus like God? Before you finish this book, I hope to prove to you that Jesus is also LORD GOD—"NOT GOD THE FATHER".

Jesus, Lord God, entered this universe by splitting TIME into. What do you mean Harvey? Adam and Eve were created about 4,000 BC (years BEFORE the BIRTH of Jesus). The world is now living approximately 2,000 AD (years AFTER the birth of Jesus). Every time you write a check or see a calendar that says 2020. You might say this is 2020 years after Jesus was born. Think about this. Jesus lived for 33 years on earth as a human like us. Therefore, it has be 1,987 years since the death of Jesus. I am trying to give you approximate dates, NOT exact dates.

Remember what I said about God's PERFECT plan. From Adam to Jesus was about 4000 years. From Jesus until today is about 2000 years. The number six denotes MAN in the Bible. God created man on the sixth day. We know the Millennium is 1000 years. That is 4000 plus 2000 plus 1000 years is 7000 years. Seven in the Bible means completion. God's PERFECT PLAN. Believe it…

As I said in the beginning of this book, the whole theme from Genesis (the beginning book in the Bible) to Revelation (the last book in the Bible) is about our Lord God Christ Jesus. He is the center of the Bible and the center of time itself.

When you think of GOD and His SON JESUS CHRIST, you cannot think in the same terms that we think here on earth. We have a beginning and an end. The most intelligent man or woman on earth cannot explain GOD OR HIS SON JESUS. GOD AND JESUS are GREATER than anything we can describe with words of our language or any other language. There are NO WORDS in ALL the languages on earth that can describe GOD AND JESUS. YOU CANNOT DO IT!!! With my earthly mind, I cannot even begin to describe GOD OR JESUS. Maybe you feel you can sufficiently describe GOD OR JESUS. I do not think so. If you think you can, you do not know the GOD OR JESUS that I know. Expand your mind to think about someone you cannot describe. That might be a beginning to describing God or Jesus? Might?

Think of the other leaders who have thousands of followers in religions. Muhammad has millions of followers and he was born April 8, 571 AD and he died. Buddha has millions of followers and he was born April 8, 563 BC and he died. You can name one religion after the other and NONE of them have a leader that split time into like Jesus. As I said in the first chapter; Is Jesus a Myth? We do not know the exact date Jesus was born. We do know it was when BC and AD came together. Yes, Jesus died like ALL the other leaders. However, UNLIKE them Jesus AROSE from the dead after three days, and He LIVES FOREVER and FOREVER. JESUS WILL NEVER DIE AGAIN. ALL the other religious leaders CANNOT say their leader rose from the dead and now lives. Jesus is the ONLY ONE that we can say, "He still LIVES".

Jesus, Lord God, in the book of Genesis help to created Adam and Eve. Jesus was not called Jesus until He was born of Mary.

St John lived longer than all the other disciples. St John also wrote Revelation, the last book in the Bible.

Go to St John 1:1 to 5 and 10 to 14:

"In the beginning was the WORD, and the WORD was with God, and the WORD <u>WAS GOD</u>. (2) The same was in the beginning with God. (3) All things were made by Him; and without Him was not anything made that was made. (4) In Him was 'LIFE'; and the 'LIFE' was the light of men. (5) And the light shinned in darkness, and the darkness comprehended it not."

(10) "He was in the world, and the world <u>WAS MADE BY HIM</u>, and the world knew Him not. (11) He came unto His own, and His own received Him not. (12) But as many as received Him, to them gave He power to become the SONS OF GOD, even to them that believed on His name. (13) Which were born, not of blood, nor of the will of the flesh, nor of the will of men, but of God. (14) AND THE 'WORD' WAS MADE FLESH, AND DWELT AMOUNG US, and we beheld His glory, the glory as of the only begotten of the Father, full of grace and truth."

St John could not call Jesus by the name of Jesus. Jesus was not called Jesus until He was born of Mary. So, St John called Jesus the WORD, and the WORD (Jesus) was with God, and the WORD (Jesus) WAS GOD. St John said the WORD (Jesus) came to the world, and the world understood Him not. He (Jesus) came to His own (Jewish people) and His own received Him NOT, but as many as received Him (Jesus), to them gave He the power to become the SONS OF GOD.

As you can plainly see in St John 1:14; "And the WORD (Jesus) was made FLESH and dwelt among us". How much clearer could St John make it? It is not just St John. There are many places in the Bible that tell us that Jesus was with God in the beginning.

I feel St John had a special relationship and vision of Jesus Christ. As I said earlier, he wrote the book of St John between 85 and 90 AD. Then, later wrote Revelation in 96 AD, which is mainly a prophecy.

John the Baptist, Jesus' cousin, was born six months BEFORE Jesus was born. Yet in St John 1:15, 17 & 18 says:

(15) "John (the Baptist) bare witness of Him (Jesus), and cried, saying, 'this was He (Jesus) of whom I spoke, He that cometh after me is preferred before me: FOR HE (Jesus) WAS BEFORE ME'. (17) For the law was given by Moses, but grace and truth came by Jesus Christ. (18) NO MAN HATH SEEN GOD AT 'ANY TIME'; the only begotten SON, which is in the bosom of the FATHER, HE (Jesus) HATH DECLARED HIM (God)."

These verses I am pointing out to you should start to make it clear that Jesus was in the beginning with God as the WORD. St John could not have used a better word than to call Jesus the WORD. Remember, Jesus was not called Jesus until He was born of Mary.

St John 15:7, Jesus says:

"If ye abide in Me (Jesus), and MY <u>WORDS</u> abide in you, you shall ask what you will, and it SHALL BE DONE UNTO YOU."

How many times in the Bible do we see Jesus speaking a WORD, and a person would be healed? How many times did Jesus teach the WORD to the disciples? He told them to go unto all the world and tell others His WORD.

Think back for a moment and realize that when Jesus (WORD), and God created the world as we know it today, they did not have a hammer, saw, level or anything you might need to build or create something. They created the world with WORDS. They spoke WORDS and things came into EXISTENCE. Genesis 1:3 to 28:

(3) "And God SAID (WORDS), let there be light and there was light. (6) And God SAID (WORDS), let there be a firmament in the midst, of the waters, and let it divide the waters from the waters. (9) And God SAID (WORDS), let the waters under the Heaven be gathered, together unto one place, and let the dry land appear; and it was so. (10) And God called the dry land earth; and the gathering together of the waters called He Seas: and God saw that it was good. (11) And God SAID (WORDS), let the earth bring forth grass, the herb yielding seed, and the fruit tree yielding fruit after his kind, whose seed is, in itself, upon the earth; and it was so. (12) ... And God saw that it was good. (14)

And God SAID (WORDS), let there be lights in the firmament of the Heaven to divide the day from the night. And let them be for signs, and for seasons, and for days and for years. (20) And God SAID (WORDS)... (24) And God SAID (WORDS)... (26) And God SAID (WORDS), let Us make man in OUR image, after OUR likeness; and let them have dominion over the fish of the sea, and over the fowl of the air, and over the cattle, and over all the earth, and over every creeping thing that creeps upon the earth. (27) So God created man in His own image, in the image of God created He him; male and female created He them. (28) And God blessed them, and God said unto them, be fruitful, and multiply, and REPLENISH the earth..."

Can you believe that God created all this with WORDS?

May I just point out for all of you that talk about cavemen and dinosaurs, you cannot REPLENISH something, if it were not there before. All of them were before Adam and Eve. For all of you that think we came from a tadpole then worked our way up to monkeys, then humans, this is the place you need to put your theory.

Even in the Old Testament David said in Psalms 107:20:

"He sent His WORD, and healed them, and delivered them from their destructions."

Wait a minute. God did not send them medicine, a doctor or health food. He sent His WORD to heal them. How can a person be healed by a WORD? God created our world with WORDS, and WE CAN HEAL WITH HIS WORDS.

The story is told about a wife that would always cut both ends of a ham off before she cooked it. Her husband asked her, "why do you do that?" She said my mother did it and my grandmother did it. He said, "why did they do it?" She said, "I do not know". The wife called her mother and asked. She, said, I do it because my mother did it. Then the wife called the grandmother and asked. The grandmother said the ham was too big for her pan. I had to cut it off. MAKE SURE YOU ARE NOT THINKING A CERTAIN WAY BECAUSE PEOPLE BEFORE YOU THOUGHT AND BELIEVED THAT WAY. MAKE SURE OF WHAT YOU THINK IS "<u>RIGHT</u>".

I believe we have <u>ONE</u>, God the Father; <u>ONE</u>, Lord Jesus Christ the Son; and <u>ONE</u>, Holy Spirit. That makes up the God head.

Can you remember me telling you in; "Is Jesus JUST a Man?" The book of Luke when Jesus was praying, and Peter, John and James saw His appearance change to white as snow. And a cloud came down and covered them, and a voice came out of the cloud saying, "this is My Beloved Son, hear Him".

If Jesus could do that as a human here on earth, you MUST feel He could do that in the Old Testament when He appeared to the prophets of old. You see, I believe EVERY word written in the Bible.

We are asking the question, was Jesus Lord God? YES, HE WAS AND IS. JESUS IS THE SON OF GOD. Do you hear me? JESUS IS THE SON OF GOD. That is NOT a question, it is a statement!

Jesus was with God when He formed the earth for Adam and Eve. St John 1:1, "In the beginning was the WORD, and the WORD was with God, and the WORD WAS GOD."

At the creation Jesus had not been born. St John did not know how to describe Jesus, so he called Him the WORD.

Then St John 1:14, "The WORD was made flesh, and dwelt among us, and we beheld His glory, the glory as of the only begotten of the Father (God), full of grace and truth."

In Genesis (2:4) JESUS was spoken of as the LORD (in Hebrew was Jehovah) GOD.

In St John (1:1) tells us JESUS was spoken of as the WORD. St John (1:10) "He (JESUS) was in the world, and the world was MADE by Him, and the world knew Him not". Then St John (1:14) "And the WORD was made flesh, and dwelt among us, (and we beheld His glory, the glory as of the only begotten of the Father) full of grace and truth".

In Exodus (6:2-3) "And God spoke unto Moses, and said unto him, I am the LORD (3) And I appeared unto Abraham, unto Isaac, and unto Jacob, by the name of God Almighty, but by my name JEHOVAH was I not known to them".

Exodus 3:13-14 says; "Moses said unto God, behold, when I come unto the children of Israel, and shall say unto them, the God of your Fathers hath sent me unto you; and they shall say to me, what is His name? What shall I say unto them? (14) God said unto Moses, 'I AM THAT I AM': and He said, thus shall thou say unto the children of Israel, I AM hath sent Me unto you".

Moving forward in the first book in the Bible, written by Moses. Genesis 1:1 Reads; "In the beginning God created the Heaven." You see in (2) "earth was without form, and void: and darkness was upon the face of the deep. And the Spirit of God moved upon the face of the waters. (3) And God said, 'Let there be light': and there was light".

You see, God did not choose to tell us what happened before all of these things started taking place. According to science Cavemen and women lived thousands of years before this. Yes, there were dinosaurs living then also. So, if you want to believe that man came from apes, that is the place you insert it. I do NOT believe that theory. If that were true, why are men not coming from apes NOW?

My belief, and I think science will back me up, a great tragedy took place on earth that destroyed ALL living people, dinosaurs and plant life. All the waters were out of control, and the earth; "was void; and darkness was upon the face of the earth". You CANNOT have life if darkness is upon the face of the earth. There would NOT be any plants, trees, and ALL vegetation would be gone. Nothing was alive. That is when God came to earth and started LIFE over again.

God did not tell us the reason the earth was in this condition.

My belief is a huge meteor (or many) came through our atmosphere and hit the earth causing dust to rise and all the waters would be uncontrollable. Darkness covered ALL the earth. Everything died, and darkness was upon the face of the earth. Everything on earth was DEAD. I believe only then is when God moved on the face of the earth to control it.

YOU CAN HAVE YOUR OWN THEORY.

Let us go back to the beginning with Adam and Eve.

Adam and Eve had two sons named Cain and Abel. Cain was jealous of Abel, so he killed him. Then came the LORD GOD walking in the Garden of Eden. He asked Cain; where is your brother, Abel? Cain answered and, said; "am I my brother's keeper? Yes, we are.

Two things to point out. Cain was TALKING to our LORD GOD. Remember no one has ever hear or seen GOD, the Father at any time. The LORD GOD drove Cain from the Garden of Eden to the land of Nod. The LORD GOD set a mark on Cain lest anyone finding him would not kill him. If they did, they would have God's vengeance seven-fold. We do not know what God's mark on Cain was.

Cain found a wife in Nod—probably one of his cousins. His children were not known to worship God.

Adam and Eve had Seth after Cain and Abel. Seth and his children begin to worship and call upon the Lord. The generations of Seth followed.

Adam had Seth at 130 and died at 930. Seth had Enos and died at 920. Enos had Cainan and died at 905. Cainan had Mahalaleel and died at 910.

DO YOU SEE A PATTERN? GOD CHOSE ONE CHILD OUT OF ALL THE CHILDREN FROM EACH GENERATION.

Mahalaleel had Jared and died at 962. Jared had Enoch and died 962. Enoch had Mathuselah and walked with God, and God took him to Heaven at 365. Mathuselah had Lamech and died at 969. Mathuselah was the oldest man in the Bible. Mathuselah was also the grandfather of Noah. Mathuselah died the year of the great flood. Lamech had Noah and died at 777. Noah was 500 and had three sons: Sham, Ham and Japheth. Noah was 600 when he finished the ark. Noah died at 950 years.

However, before the Great Flood came upon the earth, God said:

Genesis 6:1 to 8; "And it came to pass, when men begin to multiply on the face of the earth, and daughters were born unto them. (2) That the SONS OF GOD (angels) saw the daughters of men that they were fair; and they took them wives of all which they chose. (3) And the LORD said, My Spirit shall not always strive with man, FOR THAT HE ALSO IS FLESH, yet his days shall be and HUNDRED and TWENTY years. (4) There were GIANTS in the earth in those days; and also after that, when the SONS OF GOD came in unto the DAUGHTERS OF MEN, and they had children to them, the same became mighty men which were of old, men of renown. (5) And God said that the wickedness of man was great in the earth, and that every imagination of the thoughts of his heart was only evil continually. (6) And it REPENTED THE LORD THAT HE HAD MADE MAN ON THE EARTH, and it grieved Him at His heart. (7) And the LORD said, I will destroy MAN WHOM I HAVE CREATED from the face of the earth; both man, and beast, and the creeping thing, and the fowls of the air; for it REPENTETH ME THAT I HAVE MADE THEM. (8) 'But' Noah found grace in the eyes of the LORD."

Most of us know about Noah's ark. The ark was 450 feet long, 75 feet wide, 45 feet high and it had three levels/floors.

The flood came in the 600 year of Noah's life. In the second month and the seventeenth day of the month Heaven was open and the flood came. It rained for forty days and nights before stopping. The waters got fifteen feet higher than the tallest mountains, and everything on earth was covered with water. EVERYTHING that had life on earth died.

Then, Noah opened the one window in the ark and sent a dove out to find land, but she returned to the ark not finding any land for her to rest on. Noah waited seven days after the rains stopped and sent a dove out again, and this time there was an olive leaf in the dove's mouth, when it returned. He waited seven more days and sent a dove out again and it did not return. He then knew the waters were going down.

The ark ended up resting on the mountains of Ararat.

It was a hundred and fifty days before the waters returned to normal.

Then God said unto Noah in Genesis chapter 9:1, the same thing He told Adam and Eve in the Garden of Eden.

1. "And God blessed Noah and his sons, and said unto them, be fruitful, and multiply, and REPLENISH the earth."

I have told you the story of Noah to let you know that God started our Human race over again. God started our human race with Adam and Eve. Their heirs became so corrupt and evil, until He destroyed our human race and started over again with Noah and his family.

Without quoting, a particular Chapter and Verse in the Bible, we know that God has allowed our human race to exist on His earth since the flood. Notwithstanding the many times man has killed other humans in wars, murders, suicides, mistakes and all source of reasons.

We also know that sometime in the future Jesus will return to earth for the final battle with the devil and cast the devil into hell forever.

Jesus will also judge all the people on earth. I believe according to the Bible the good people that love God will live with Jesus here on earth for a thousand years. There will be peace, love and no sinning at that time.

You need to read all the chapters of 21 and 22 of Revelation.

Revelation 22:1 to 5; "And he (angel) showed me a pure river of water of life, clear as crystal, and proceeding out of the throne of God and of the Lamb. (2) In the midst of the street of it, and on either side of the river, was there the tree of life, which bare twelve manner of fruits, and yielded her fruit every month: and the leaves of the tree were for the healing of the nations. (3) And there shall be no more curse: but the throne of God and of the Lamb shall be in it; and His servants shall serve Him. (4) And they shall see His face; and His name shall be on their foreheads. (5) And there shall be no night there; and they need no candle, neither light of the sun; for the LORD GOD giveth them light: and THEY SHALL REIGN FOR EVER AND EVER. (6) And he said unto me, these sayings are faithful and true: and the LORD GOD of the holy prophets sent His angel to show unto His servants the things which must shortly be done. (7) 'Behold, I come quickly; blessed is he that keeps the sayings of the prophecy of this book'."

St John saw these things and hear them. Please read all of Chapters 21 and 22 of Revelation.

Whatever happens during and after this, I am sure it will be wonderful. We will be with the LORD GOD, and that is all I need. What do you think? Is that all you need?

Think how PERFECT God's plan is. Adam was created at 4,000 BC (before Christ). Jesus was born at BC and AD (before Christ Jesus and after Christ). Since Christ died it has been about 2,000 years. This is 2020 AD. After the judgement we live with Christ for a thousand years (PLUS).

4000 BC – Adam was created

BC and AD – Christ was born and died

2000 AD – since Christ was born

1000 AD – we will live with Christ on earth

4000 plus 2000, plus 1000 equals 7000 years.

Throughout the Bible seven means completion. Throughout the Bible three means the Godhead (Father, Son and Holy Spirit). Throughout the Bible six means man (remember in Genesis God created Adam on the sixth day). Remember in the Bible, when creation was complete, God rested on the seventh day? Throughout the Bible twelve means God's chosen people—twelve tribe of Israel, twelve disciples and 144,000 Jews returning to God (12X12); before the return of Christ.

Numbers play a very, important part to God. Our entire human race lives by numbers. Our computers, calendars (days, months and years), hours we work, amount we get paid, interest paid, rent, payment on our properties, miles we travel, years we live, hours in a day and on and on.

The last spaceship we sent into outer space had to be shot from earth at a certain second of the day. That is so it could meet up with our space station in outer space. Think for a moment. Everything in our live is with numbers.

That is the reason God has a PERFECT plan for our lives. No, we do not know the exact time and date that Jesus will return to earth for us. We DO NOT KNOW WHEN HE WILL RETURN to earth, only God the Father knows the time and date. According to our calendar and the prophecies in the Bible, I would think it is getting very, close to the time. However, I do not know. Only God the Father knows the time and date when Jesus will return to earth for us.

I just saw a minister on TV in Ohio arrested for standing on the street and singing a song to Jesus. Yes, this new virus that is going on, and he did not have a mask on. God PLEASE heal our land before all humans have gone mad.

The way I understand the Bible is just before Christ returns to earth there will be SEVEN years of tribulations (abomination of desolation). Three and a half that are bad. Then three and a half years that except the Lord shortened no man shall be saved. St Mark 13:19-20:

(19) "For in those days shall be affliction, such as was not from the beginning of the creation which God created unto this time, neither shall be. (20) And except that the Lord had shortened those days, no flesh should be saved: but for the elect's sake, whom He (Lord) hath chosen, He hath shortened the days."

St Mark is describing the end of the second three and a half years. St Mark 13:24 to 27:

"But in those days, after that tribulation, the sun shall be darkened, and the moon shall not give her light. (25) And the stars of Heaven shall fall, and the powers that are in Heaven shall be shaken. (26) And then shall they see the SON OF MAN (Jesus) coming in the clouds with great power and glory. (27) And then shall He (Jesus) send His angels and shall gather, together His elect from the four winds, from the uttermost part of the earth to the uttermost part of Heaven."

Then as I told you earlier, no one knows the time of the return of Jesus, except God the Father St Mark 13:32-33:

(32) "But of that day and that hour knows no man, no, not the angels which are in Heaven, neither the Son (Jesus), but the FATHER. (33) Take ye heed, watch and pray; for ye know NOT when the time is."

No one knows the TIME except GOD the FATHER!

Like in the days of Noah, no one wanted to hear are believe, what Noah was saying about the FLOOD coming. Many of us are like that today. It is a shame because the quotation above from St Mark is REAL. Yes, it will happen.

I am not trying to frighten you. I am trying to tell you what is going to take place in the future. Please listen to me. This is written in the Bible. This is TRUE. You do not have to be frighten. All you need to do is accept Jesus Christ as your personal Savior. Believe Jesus is the true SON of GOD. The name of JESUS is above ALL other names. Believe that God controls the earth and the Heavens. If you truly, believe, you do not need to be afraid. God will take care of you.

Now let us talk a little more about numbers. I said three represents the Godhead, and six represents man. During the tribulation (seven years), a man will come forward calling himself the antichrist. Well, what do you think he will do? He will say he is Christ. Now you know the reason we say he will have the mark of 666. Remember three stands for the Godhead, and six stands for man. He will try to say he is god—666. Stop and think about that for a minute. Six stands for man, and three stands for the Godhead. Six three times means the antichrist is a man. Believe it!!!

I might write a book on Revelation (the last book in the Bible) next. Revelation 1:3 says: "The Revelation of Jesus Christ, which God gave unto him, to show unto His servants things which must shortly come to pass; and He sent and signified it by His angel unto His servant John. (2) Who bare record of the WORD of GOD, and of the testimony of JESUS CHRIST, and of all things that he saw. (3) Blessed is he that readeth, and they that hear the WORDS of this prophecy, and keep those things which are written therein: for the TIME IS AT HAND."

Everyone that is reading this book and loves Jesus Christ as your personal Savior needs to pray daily to Him and be ready when Jesus returns. This is NOT a game. This is NOT a movie. This is REAL LIFE. Jesus is going to return TO EARTH for His people. WE NEED TO BE READY WHEN HE DOES. As I showed you in the Bible, ONLY God the Father knows the time and date. I feel in my heart IT WILL BE SOON.

This world has become so corrupt and evil until I cannot believe God would allow it to last to much longer. This world has become like Sodom and Gomorrah when the LORD destroyed them. Genesis 19:24 "Then the LORD rained upon Sodom and upon Gomorrah brimstone and fire from the LORD out of Heaven."

Also, II Peter 2:6: "And turning the cities of Sodom and Gomorrah into ashes condemned them with an overthrow, making them an ensample unto those that after should live ungodly."

This is what God is going to do with this world if we do not change our ways. It seems the world IS NOT going to change its way. It is so sad. This world could be so beautiful just the way God created it.

To Summorize:

Is Jesus God?

Let us read again St John 1:1: "In the beginning was the WORD, and the WORD was with God, and the WORD WAS GOD."

Notice in the verse above, it says the WORD WAS GOD. The WORD was Jesus in the beginning with God the Father. Remember, He was not called Jesus until He was born of Mary. You might say who is the WORD? Let us look again at St John 1:14:

"And the WORD was made FLESH, and dwelt among us, (and we beheld His glory, the glory as of the only begotten of the Father), full of grace and truth."

Can this be any more, clearer to you? St John could not call the WORD Jesus. He was not called Jesus until He was born of Mary four thousand years later. I can show you a hundred or more places in the Bible where it says Jesus was in the beginning with God the Father.

If Jesus (WORD) is the SON OF GOD, and He was in the beginning with God when God created Adam and Eve, then that is the reason St John called Jesus GOD. So, I feel we can call Jesus the SON OF GOD and, also call Him LORD GOD. What do you think?

THERE is <u>ONE</u> GOD the FATHER, and <u>ONE</u> SON OF GOD (Jesus), and <u>ONE</u> HOLY SPIRIT. That is what the Bible says, and THAT IS WHAT I BELIEVE.

So, the answer to the third question I posed in the beginning of this book: Is Jesus God? The answer is yes. 'Not' GOD the Father but LORD God. He is LORD GOD mentioned in Genesis 2:4 and many other verses. Notice that Moses says in the first chapter of Genesis that GOD made; HEAVEN, the EARTH and all the other things ON EARTH for six days and rested on the seventh day.

Then Moses in Genesis 2:4 begins to summary ALL the creation that God had worked on in chapter one. I feel if we just get in our thinking that GOD the Father and LORD GOD, Jehovah were together when God the Father said; "let US make man in OUR image, after OUR likeness;" Genesis 1:26, our thinking WILL BE CLEARER.

Notice that Moses in the summary of creation, just mentioned the THIRD day and the SIXTH day of creation; Genesis 2:5 to 7.

Then, Moses writes in Genesis 2:7; "that the LORD GOD formed man of the dust of the ground and breathed into his nostrils the breath of LIFE; and man became a living soul."

Now let us turn to St John 1:3,4 "ALL things were made by HIM (Jesus); and without Him was not anything made that was made. (4) In HIM WAS 'LIFE'; and the 'LIFE' was the light of men."

I AM "NOT" TAKING ANYTHING AWAY FROM "GOD THE FATHER". LORD GOD CANNOT DO ANYTHING WITHOUT GOD THE FATHER. "US" IN GENESIS 1:26; AND "LORD GOD" IN GENESIS 2:4; AND "WORD" IN ST JOHN 1:1: JUST MEANS THAT GOD THE FATHER AND GOD THE SON WERE TOGETHER IN THE BEGINNING WHEN THEY CREATED THE EARTH, HEAVEN AND ADAM AND EVE.

Maybe that will make it more clear to you. I hope so.

I have already shown you in St John 1:14 that the WORD (Jesus) was made flesh and dwelled among us here on earth.

I have already shown you in St John 1:18; "NO MAN HATH SEEN GOD AT ANY TIME; the only begotten Son, which is in the bosom of the Father, HE HATH DECLARED HIM." IN OTHER WORDS, JESUS HAS REVEALED GOD THE FATHER UNTO ALL OF US.

Let us talk about Moses for a moment. Moses was God's agent in delivering the Hebrews from the slave labor camps of Egypt and molding them into the nation of Israel. Moses was born near the Egyptian capital, Memphis, at the time of oppressive measures against Hebrews were being intensified. Pharaoh had decreed that all male Hebrew babies were to be murdered. Moses was saved by his mother. She put him in a basket in the Nile River where the princess walked. The princess took and raised him in the Egyptian court. Moses always had a sense of justice for the Hebrew people.

One day, when he saw an Egyptian beating a Hebrew, he struck him and killed him. Moses fled to Midian. He married a daughter of Jethro, the priest, and settled into the life of a shepherd. God confronted Moses there and commissioned the reluctant, stammer, excuse maker to go back to Egypt and lead the Hebrew people out of captivity. Moses persuaded Aaron, his brother, to talk for him.

Pharaoh would not allow his slaves to leave. However, after many plagues he was forced to release his slave laborers. The Hebrew slaves followed Moses eastward toward Suez. You have heard the story of how Pharaoh changed his mind and sent his army after them. Moses, lead his people through the sea, but when the army came after them, the army were all drowned.

Then they wondered in the wilderness for forty years with their complaining and unbelieving while Moses was trying to make them into a nation of believing in God. At Mount Sinai God, through Moses, made a covenant in writing with Israel. Moses was truly a great man. After 40 years of bring his people to the edge of the Promised Land, Moses died because he disobeyed one of God's commands. Moses is spoken of in nearly every book in the Bible.

The first FIVE books in the Bible were written by Moses.

Hundreds of years before the birth of Jesus, the Lord said in Exodus for Moses to bring the children of Israel out of bondage, Exodus 33:17 to 20:

(17) "And the LORD said unto Moses, I will do this thing also that thou hast spoken; for thou hast found grace in my sight, and I know thee by name. (18) And he

said, I beseech thee, show me thou glory. (19) And He said, I will make all My goodness pass before thee, and I will proclaim the name of the LORD before thee; and I will be gracious to whom I will be gracious, and will show mercy on whom I will show mercy. (20) AND HE SAID, THOU CANST NOT SEE MY FACE: FOR THERE SHALL 'NO' MAN SEE ME, AND LIVE."

Remember, Jesus said; "NO MAN HAS SEEN GOD AT ANY TIME". In the above verse the LORD GOD allowed Moses to see the back of Him. Moses could NOT see His face and live.

GOD THE FATHER, and LORD GOD (the SON OF GOD), and the SPIRIT OF GOD are a lot more then we as humans can ever begin to understand. THEY ARE GODLY, HEAVENLY and 'UNSPEAKABLE', and SO 'MUCH' MORE.

Philip, one of the twelve, asked Jesus to show them the Father and they would be satisfied. Then St John 14:9-10 says: "(9) Jesus said unto him, have I been so long with you, and yet hath thou not known Me, Philip? HE THAT HAST SEEN ME HAST SEEN THE FATHER; then how sayest you then, show us the Father? (10) Believe thou not that I AM IN MY FATHER, and the FATHER IN ME? The words that I speak unto you I speak NOT OF MYSELF; but the Father that DWELLETH IN ME, He does the works."

I AM GOING TO MAKE A LOUD BOLD STATEMENT. ANY TIME IN THE BIBLE YOU SEE ANY PERSON TALK TO GOD, THEY WERE TALKING TO THE LORD GOD—THE SON OF GOD (JESUS).

You can have your belief, and I will have mine. I hope this makes you study the Bible more to understand the word.

Back to Genesis 2:7: "And the LORD GOD formed man of the dust of the ground and BREATHED INTO HIS NOSTRILS THE BREATH OF LIFE; and man became a living soul."

The word LORD in Hebrew is interpreted as JEHOVAH. The meaning is, "He is the self-existent One who REVEALS Himself." This name is, itself, an advance upon the name "God" (El, Elah, Elohim) which suggests certain attributes of Deity, as strength, etc., rather than His essential being.

Remember on the cross Jesus said, "E-li, E-li, la-ma sa-bach-tha-ni? That is to say; My God, My God, why hast Thou forsaken Me?" Jesus called on GOD the FATHER. We know that God the Father CANNOT LOOK upon sin. Jesus took ALL the sins of the world upon Himself on the cross. That is the reason God, the Father, turned His face away from Jesus.

It is significant that the first appearance of the name Jehovah in scripture is at the creation of man. It was God (Elohim) who said, "let US make man in OUR image" (Genesis 1:26) However, when man, as in the second chapter of Genesis, has filled the scene and become dominant over creation, it is the LORD GOD Jehovah (Elohim) who acts. This clearly indicates a special relationship of Deity, in His Jehovah characteristic role, to man, and all scripture emphasizes that.

Jehovah is distinctly the redemption name of Deity. When sin entered and redemption became necessary, it was Jehovah (Elohim) who sought the sinning ones (Genesis 3:9 to 13) and with "coats of skins, clothed them" Genesis 3:21). A beautiful type of righteousness provided by the LORD GOD through sacrifice (Roman 3:21,22). The first distinct revelation of Himself by the name of Jehovah was in connection with the redemption of the covenant with His people out of EGYPT (Exodus 3:14 to 16):

(14) "And God said unto Moses, I AM THAT I AM: and He said, thus shall thou say unto the children of Israel, I AM hath sent me unto you. (15) And God said moreover unto Moses, thus shall thou say unto the children of Israel, the LORD GOD of your fathers, the God of Abraham, the God of Isaac, and the God of Jacob, hath sent me unto you: this is My Name for ever, and is My memorial unto all generations. (16) Go, and

gather the elders of Israel together, and say unto them. The LORD GOD of your fathers, the God of Abraham, of Isaac, and of Jacob, APPEARED unto me, saying, I have surely visited you, and seen that which is done to you in Egypt: (17) and I have said, I will bring you up out of the affliction of Egypt."

One more example that Jesus was God in St John 10:22 to 39 (please read). Jesus went to Jerusalem for the feast of dedication, and it was winter. He walked in the temple on Solomon's porch. The Jews were round about Him and they asked why do you make us doubt? Are You the Christ, tell us plainly now? Jesus said, I told you before and you believe Me not. Jesus said the works I do in My Father's name, they should tell you who I am? Jesus said in Verse 30; "I AND MY FATHER ARE ONE. (31) Then the Jews took up stones again to stone Him. (33) The Jews answered Him, saying, for a good work we stone thee not; but for blasphemy; and because that thou, being a man, MAKEST THYSELF GOD. (38) But if I do, though, ye believe not Me, believe the works; that you may know, and believe, that the FATHER IS IN ME, AND I IN HIM". Again, they wanted to stone Jesus. He escaped out of their hands.

Trust me, I am not trying to get you to think like me. I am trying to get you to see what is written in the Bible. It is spelled out. It is clear. It is something you should look at. It is all about studying the Bible more.

I just want to lay it all out in a way that you might say, "yes, that is possible". That might be true. Maybe; "yes, I believe that". The Bible is an outstanding book. It covers a period of 6000 years (4000 before Jesus, and 2,000 years after Christ). It even talks about 1000 years in our future.

We need to go into this more...

I need to write another 500 pages just to begin to tell you how wonderful Jesus really is. He is EVERYTHING to the world and to me. If only I could worship and praise Him every moment for the rest of my life, it would NOT be enough.

PS: Last night 7-29-20 I was in pain all night. I prayed and thanked the Lord for healing me. Today 7-30-20 I am out of pain. Thank you, Jesus. Yes, He healed me. Jesus is wonderful!!!

Dear LORD, I want to take a moment, not to ask for <u>anything</u> from You, but simply say thank You for all I have, or will have.

Everyone DIES, but not everyone LIVES.

I live alone in my condo, but many times I can start singing, "Oh, how I LOVE Jesus, Oh, how I love JESUS". Then I can feel the Spirit of the Lord with me, and start crying and worshiping the Lord. Jesus said in St John 14:16-17:

"I will pray the Father, and He shall give you another Comforter, that He may abide with you FOR EVER; (17) Even the Spirit of truth; whom the world cannot receive, because it sees Him not, neither knows Him: but ye know Him; for He dwelleth with you and SHALL BE IN YOU."

I hope you know Jesus the way I know Him. I cannot praise Him enough.

Are you convinced that Jesus is not a myth? Are you convinced that Jesus is greater than any Man that has ever lived on earth? Are you convinced that Jesus is LORD GOD mentioned in Genesis? Are you convinced that Jesus is the one John was talking about when he said, "In the beginning was the WORD"? Are you convinced that Jesus did ALL the miracles mentioned in the Bible? Are you convinced that Jesus came back from the dead after three days? Are you convinced that Jesus is the SON OF GOD? If you believe all of this and accept Jesus Christ as your Personal Savior, then some day I will meet you in Heaven with our LORD. Please let me know some way that you read this book.

May the Lord bless you, and all your loved ones. Amen.

Last Thoughts:

How LARGE is Heaven?

Let us start here on Earth. First EVERYTHING here has an END. Humans, plants, animals, etc. Humans are promised 120 years after the Great Flood. None of us now get to 120 (Genesis 6:3). Most plants last for one season. Storms last for days or weeks. However, EVERYTHING has an END. You try and name people, animals, plants, fish, insects, etc. and see if they have an END? Some sea life lives for many, many years, but they have an END. Even trees sometimes live for hundreds of years, but they have an END. ALL life on earth has an END. Did you name any life that does not have an END?

God's Son, Jesus, came to earth to show us how to live and worship God. Jesus was teaching His disciples how to pray. In Matthew 6:9 "After this manner therefore pray ye: Our Father which art in Heaven, hallowed be Thy Name. (10) Thy kingdom come, THY WILL BE DONE IN EARTH, AS IT IS IN HEAVEN".

Our EARTH is very uniquely created. Some science says the EARTH is 15 billion years old, and maybe it is? However, our world, as we know it today, is approximately 6,000 years old.

The Heaven or Heavens excite me, because once you see there is no limit to how huge they are you MUST realize there is a God that controls all the Heavens.

Stars are like our sun—they glow. They probably have planets around them like our sun. Stars are not like our nine plus planets. You cannot see their planets when you gaze at the stars at night with you naked eyes.

There are some stars that died, disappeared hundreds of years ago, and we are still getting the light from them. They must have been trillions of Light Years away—not miles? How can that be? Remember, I said light is the fastest thing we have here on earth. How can we still be getting light from some of these stars that are no longer there? Because the Heavens DO NOT HAVE AN END. Just like GOD DOES NOT HAVE AN

END, and HE DOES NOT HAVE A BEGINNING ALSO.

In our world as we know it, we have our Sun, earth, moon, nine plus planets PLUS the Milky Way. This is considered our Heaven in Genesis first chapter—Heaven NOT Heavens. I wrote a whole chapter about this in my book, "Bible Understanding plus Circle of Love". Moses did not start talking about Heavens, until Genesis second chapter.

Now look at God and Heavens. THEY HAVE NO ENDING AND NO BEGINNING. That is more than I can comprehend. That is the reason I said, I do not believe you or anyone can explain GOD with ALL the words we have here on earth.

Maybe I will try and attempt to explain Heaven? Our Moon is approximately 240,000 miles from earth. Our Sun is about 93 million miles from earth. After that we will have to start measuring with Light Years. What does that mean? Light is the fastest thing we have on earth. A Light Year is how far a light can travel in a year. Light travels 186,000 miles in one second, 11 million miles in one minute and 678 million miles in an hour. ONE LIGHT YEAR IS 5,878,499,810,000 miles a light will travel in one year. Yes, that is 5 trillion, 878 billion miles in one year. Our Milky Way is 58,784,998,100,000,000 miles wide. Have I made my point?

Do you understand what I am trying to tell you? God and Jesus have NO ENDING. God had no beginning.

The closest Galaxy to our Milky Way Galaxy is Andromeda gal and that is 2,200,000 Light Years away—NOT MILES from our Milky Way Galaxy.

It is easy to describe everything here on earth, but when it comes to Heaven we cannot. I do not believe there is anyone on earth can comprehend, understand the true greatness of the Heavens or GOD. I cannot.

WE HAVE NO LANGUAGE ON EARTH TO DESCRIBE THE HEAVENS AND OUR 'GOD THE FATHER'.

Most all the atheist that I have met are wonderful peoples. If you were in unspeakable pain and hurting very, very badly, you would call on someone to help you. That is God.

If you are truly an atheist and do not believe in God, please explain to me how space does not have an end. Please explain to me how trillions of stars in Heaven are spinning and moving around and there is complete harmony in our universe.

Heaven is not where you go a trillion miles and there is a wall to show the end. There is no end. How can that be? I guess we will have to ask God. He created all of it. He looks after all of it. God is the one that has NO BEGINNING AND NO ENDING. I know this is hard for some of us to except and believe. IT IS TRUE. Try and tell yourself IT IS TRUE.

When I die and there was no God, that would be BAD. HOWEVER, WHEN I DIE AND THERE IS THE ONE GOD, I WILL BE GLAD I BELIEVED IN HIM. I WILL BE HAPPY BECAUSE I CAN LIVE WITH HIM SOME DAY FOREVER AND EVER.

I am the first to say, I DO NOT understand everything that God has said or does. However, if you DO NOT believe in the Bible or a SUPREME POWER, it is going to be hard for you to accept some of the things said IN THIS BOOK.

No army or ANYONE can STOP THE TRUTH OF GOD'S OR JESUS' WORDS.

St John 3:13 "No man hath ascended up to Heaven, but He that CAME DOWN from Heaven, even the Son of man (Jesus) which is in Heaven". NOW...

"JESUS IS THE LIGHT"

Let us start with St John 1:3 "All things were made by Him (Jesus), and without Him was not anything made that was made. (4) IN HIM WAS LIFE; AND THE "LIFE" WAS THE "LIGHT" OF MEN. (5) And the

LIGHT shineth in darkness (earth); and the darkness comprehended it not".

Now let us switch to Revelation. The 21st and 22nd chapters describe the new Heaven that God is preparing for all Christians. Please take the time to read those two chapters. St John described the things to come in Revelation 21:22 to 24 "And I saw no temple therein: for the LORD GOD Almighty and the LAMB are the temple of it. (23) And the city had no need of the sun, neither the moon, to shine in it: FOR THE GLORY OF GOD DID LIGHTEN IT, and the LAMB IS THE "LIGHT" THEREOF. (24) And the nations of them which are saved shall walk in the "LIGHT" OF IT: and the kings of this earth do bring their glory and honor unto it".

Also, Revelation 22:5 "And there shall be no night there; and they need no candle, neither light of the sun; for the LORD GOD giveth them "LIGHT": AND THEY SHALL REIGN FOR EVER AND EVER".

Throughout the Old and New Testaments men of God have spoken of the Lord (Jesus) being a "LIGHT" to them. King David said the Lord was a "LIGHT" unto his path.

Remember before Saul accepted the Lord as his Savior, he saw a great "LIGHT" that made him blind for a time. The Lord told him to go in the city and a certain man would pray for him so he could receive his site? The great "LIGHT" was Jesus. The Lord changed Saul's name to Paul, and he wrote about half of the New Testament.

Why can't all of us see that Jesus is our "LIGHT"? He is the One that changed my life. I hope He is the One that has changed your life. If you pray to Him, He will be the "LIGHT" for your life. Jesus is going to be our only "LIGHT" in the New Heaven that is being prepared for us now. Can you even think for a moment if the sun did not come up tomorrow or the moon did not shine? However, in Revelation 21:23 it is written there will be "NO NEED OF THE SUN, NEITHER OF THE MOON".

Whyooo! The Glory of God, and Lamb of God, are the only "LIGHT" we will ever need. As a Christian, just think about that for a few minutes. We are going to live with Jesus for ever and ever, and we will see His face. No more sickness. No more dying. We only have day "LIGHT". I LOVE YOU, Jesus, and I LOVE that reality.

ENJOY THESE SAYS:

There are only two ways to live your life. One is as though nothing is a miracle. The other is as though everything is a miracle. Albert Einstein

What we think, we become. Buddha

Knowing yourself is the beginning of all wisdom. Aristotle

Life is short, live it. Love is rare, grab it. Anger is sad, dump it. Fear is awful, face it. Memories are sweet, cherish them. Zig Ziglar

We would accomplish many, more things, if we did not think of them as impossible. Vince Lombardi

Accept what is, let go of what was, and have faith in what will be.

One day I would like to turn on the News and hear: "there is Peace on Earth".

Aspire to inspire before you expire.

SHORT STORIES:

MIDNIGHT

After getting older, I suddenly realize God has allowed me to see many MIDNIGHTS in my life. Now I look at MIDNIGHT as a beginning of a new day. However, now I have something to look forward to—a new morning light in my life. I look forward to a new idea. I look forward to something great happening in my life. I look forward to a new beginning in my life. I know that just a few more hours and there will be light. Yes, light that you can see things that you could not see in the dark. Even though it is dark at MIDNIGHT, I know in just a few more hours there will be light.

I have always had a problem sleeping. Many nights I have watched the moon and stars and wondered when I could find sleep. Now I look at it through a different vision of life. I tell myself things are going to be great when the light comes. I tell myself something wonderful is going to happen when the light comes. Even though I have a sleep aide, when I wake in the morning light, there is a feeling, I did not have in the dark a few hours ago. It is a new day. A day I can start anew. A new day I can thank God for allowing me to have. One day older that many people do not have.

MIDNIGHT is a new beginning for me. It is a start of a new day. It is the start of things I have always wanted in my life, but I never had. My newly found friend is faith. That tells me to hold on until the wisdom or light comes. It is MIDNIGHT and I know in a few hours there will be light. Even though the sun is 93 million miles away, it will rise in the East. Just like it has for thousands of years. Faith inspires me that, when the light comes, it will be a new day. Yes, a day that God has promised me would bring light.

When MIDNIGHT comes now, I smile and say tomorrow is going to be a new day. A new day I know God is going to give me some of the things I have asked for. A new day that I can look forward to. A wonderful day that God has given me. A beautiful day that I can say I am one more day older.

YES, MIDNIGHT IS THE BEGINNING OF A NEW DAY.

NIGHT PRAYER

Now I lay me down to SLEEP

Only I CANNOT go to sleep

I pray the Lord my soul to KEEP

Yes, I know He WILL

If I should die before I WAKE

I pray the Lord my soul to TAKE

I KNOW He will (Amen 3 AM)

LOVE TO SHARE

It seems I have a million pounds of LOVE. Even though, I have just used a pound. How can I find a way to use this before I pass?

Maybe through a gift, a song or a word? Wait. I need God's help to do this. Yes, I cannot do it on my own. God is LOVE, and that is where the million pounds came.

LOVE we give away is the only LOVE we keep.

Now, please, help me to give it away before I pass.

This is the only thing will make my life complete.

So, please God, help me to make my life complete for You.

WORRYING IS LIKE A ROCKINGCHAIR

You keep rocking, worrying working at it.

By worrying you never get to where you WANT to go.

A wise man said, "over 90% of the things you worry about NEVER come to past".

Why are we spending over 90% of our time worrying, when it is not going to happen? Everyone is going to worry some, however, try to worry less.

With everything happening today, it is hard NOT to worry. I know.

I do not believe God wants us to worry. Give the problem to Him. Let God work it out. He is the ONLY One that can.

Ignore those who say just get over it. Healing is a process.

WITH GOD NOTHING IS IMPOSSIBLE.

I John 4:18 "There is no fear in love; but PERFECT LOVE cast out fear; because fear hath torment. He that fears is not made perfect in love".

DO IT NOW

Listen to the wind, it talks.

Listen to the silence, it speaks.

Listen to your heart, it knows.

One day you will wake up, and there will not be any more time, to do the things you have always wanted to do.

I recorded a song years ago called "Wasted Years".

It went like this; "Wasted Years, Wasted Years, Oh, how foolish. As you walk on in darkness and fear. Turn around, turn around God is calling. He is calling you from a life of Wasted Years."

DO IT NOW…

FOR YOUR LOVED ONE

I can go hours without talking to you, minutes without seeing you, but NOT a second goes by, I do not think about you.

MANKIND'S FIRST SIN
"DISOBEDIENCE TO GOD"

God placed Adam and Eve in the Garden of Eden and told them they could do anything they wished to do, except EAT from one tree in the middle of the garden. They could eat from ANY of the other trees in the garden. They did not have to work to grow them. All they had to do is enjoy them.

They could look upon each other naked with God's approval. They could do what humans do and call "what comes naturally" with God's approval.

They might have lived forever. Who knows? Adam did live 930 years and died (Genesis 5:5).

I know God said to Adam in Genesis 2:17, "but of the tree of knowledge of good and evil, thou shalt not eat of it; FOR IN THE DAY that thou eat thereof THOU SHALT SURELY DIE". Then Genesis 3:2 to 5 the serpent said to Eve, you will not DIE. Then the serpent said to Eve in verse 5. "For God doth know that in the DAY you eat thereof, then your eyes shall be opened, and you shall be as gods, knowing good from evil". God told Adam in the DAY, and the serpent told Eve in the DAY.

You might say God did not keep His word—you would be WRONG. Adam did die at 930 years old. Adam might have lived FOREVER.

Now let us look in II Peter 3:8; Peter said, "believed, be not ignorant OF THIS ONE THING, that one DAY is with the Lord as a THOUSAND years, and a THOUSAND years as a DAY". Adam died at 930 years old, and ALL the other people before and Great Flood with Noah DIED within a THOUSAND YEARS. The oldest person that lived before the FLOOD was Methuselah. He was 969 years old and he died the year of the FLOOD. He was Noah's grandfather. Look in the book of Genesis and see how long all the other lived.

God caused the flood to happen because mankind had become so EVIL. Even the "sons of God" (angels) were having sex with the daughters of man and the Lord repented that He had made man (Genesis 1:1 to 7) "And the Lord said, 'I will destroy man whom I have created from the face of the earth; both man and beast…for it repenteth Me that I have made them'." Verse 8, "But Noah found grace in the eyes of the Lord". That was the reason for the Great Flood.

After the flood God just promised Mankind 120 years to live. None of us are lucky enough to live 120 years. Many men of God lived to almost 1,000 years before the Flood.

If Mankind (Adam and Eve) did not DISOBEY God, who knows how long all of us could have lived?

A SEED MUST BE PLANTED TO GROW

You can put a seed on your table for 50 years and it will not grow. However, after 50 years you plant it, and it will grow. This is the way God created a seed. The seed will always produce what type of seed it is (Genesis 1:11,12). This is a miracle within itself.

Jesus also used a seed as and example to His disciples in St Matthew 17:19,20: "Then came the disciples to Jesus apart, and said, why could we not case the devil out of the child? (20) And Jesus said unto them, because of your unbelief: for verily I say unto you, 'if ye have faith as a grain of a mustard seed, ye shall say unto this mountain, remove hence to yonder place; and it shall remove; and nothing shall be impossible unto you'."

You see, Jesus was telling them that with a little amount of faith like a mustard seed, one of the smallest seeds on earth, you can move mountains.

WHAT HAPPENED TO MY LIFE?

When I think that over half my life has passed and gone, what have I done in this large world and round?

Have I done things that will last, or have I done things I am not proud of?

Have I looked to my Maker for guidance, or watched my life slipping away?

Am I serving my Lord from on high?

When I feel everything is passing me by?

Is it death to hide the desires within, or play them out for our own advantage?

Does God demand we work for Him? But fast my answer replied.

God does not force us to work for Him, but would it not be nice doing things that will last?

Yes, I know talents hide with inside.

If only I had followed the small voice saying. "go this way or that".

Then my life would have been something, and not just passing me by.

I know what God wants of me, why did I not provide?

Even though I know God has thousands of Angels that would provide for Him.

Yet I am one small voice that could have provided a book, a song or poem.

Why, why I must ask myself.

When my heart brakes to do something great for You.

Will I ever have the chance to see my total dreams come true?

Even though most of my life has passed and gone?

LORD, PLEASE, LET ME DO SOMETHING GREAT FOR YOU.

IF ONLY WITH A WORD A BOOK OR SONG, AMEN.

WHO IS THAT MAN IN THE MIRROR?

I see him, but it is not me.

I am 35 and he is 70.

How can that be?

Mirrors should show who you are?

That is not true in this case.

Can I bring him out of the mirror?

And tell him he is not 70, he is 35.

Is that possible?

What happened between 35 and 70?

Could I ask him if he lived a good life?

What happened between 35 and 70?

Did I just wake up from a long dream?

Was I really living my life?

Was I just surviving?

My prayer is, Lord let me live my life, from now to 100 or until the end.

YOU ARE UNIQUE

Just think when your mother produced an egg, there were millions of sperm trying to attach themselves to the egg. Very, likely just one of those sperms attached itself, and that one sperm helped to decide the color of your eyes, hair, skin, speech, hearing, smell, etc. That one sperm can also tell if you are healthy or sick. If you are black, white or brown.

Your blood line comes from that one sperm, or from your father. That tells if you are Jewish, Gentile or any other heritage.

This is the reason you are unique. God knew which sperm, out of millions, was going to attach itself to make a baby. The same way God knows the number of hairs on your head. The same way God knows when just one small sparrow falls in the forest.

God even knows what you are thinking.

ALL ABOUT JESUS & A LITTLE ABOUT ME

I thought I might close this book by telling a lot about what Jesus has done in my life, and a little about me.

When I was just seven years old in a small Church of God in Stockton, CA., I fell on my knees and gave my life to Jesus. I can still feel how wonderful it was then.

Sorry, but I need to tell you a few things in my life before. Born in Atlanta, Georgia at Grady Hospital. My father walked out on my mother when I was two months old. My brother was eight, and my sister was four years old. My mother was on her own and had three small children. I can remember my grandmother taking care of us while mom worked three jobs to buy food, clothing, rent, etc. Yes, we were really, poor. Mom would not accept welfare from the government.

I could tell you hundreds of things that happened in my childhood, but this book is about Jesus not me.

Just a few more things for you to know. When I was about three, dad took mom to court to get custody of my sister and me. He DID NOT win. That is the reason we traveled so much. I went to twelve different schools up to the 8th grade.

I stopped going to church until I was about fifteen. That is when I really got into working for Riverside

Church of God in Atlanta. Two years later we had a traveling minister come to our church for a meeting. Little did I know his daughter was to become my wife.

At eighteen I joined the Air Force Reserve for seven months. My future wife's father asked if I wanted to work for his church that he was starting in Louisville, Kentucky. I said "yes". Then I got an honorable discharge and started working for the church (Calvary Cathedral) to become an ordained minister. After three years of his daughter and I dating, we got married.

Working for God's church was the most wonderful experience of my life. After being married for a long time and having a wonderful son named Todd Lynn Hames, we got a divorce. She moved to Nashville and I want into real estate.

I wanted to move to Florida and retire. The girl I was dating wanted to go with me. That was November 2013. In February 2014 she found out she had breast cancer. After fitting the cancer for seven years, she passed on to Heaven in January 2020.

In the last seven years I have found a closeness to God that I have never, ever, ever experienced in my life.

When I read John 3:16; "For God so LOVED the world, that He gave His only begotten Son, that whosoever believeth in Him should not perish, but have everlasting life." Verses like this have a NEW meaning for me. I LOVE You, JESUS.

I could almost write a book on all the SHORT STORIES.

Hope you have enjoyed this book. Please let me know if you did.

harvey@harveyhames.com

www.harveyhames.com

J. Harvey Hames

(502) 639-2182 cell

Delray Beach, FL 33484

Thank you and God bless you…

www.ingramcontent.com/pod-product-compliance
Lightning Source LLC
LaVergne TN
LVHW011956070526
838202LV00054B/4933